EFFECTIVE WRITING SKILLS FOR PUBLIC RELATIONS

PR in Practice Series

Published in association with the Institute of Public Relations
Consultant Editor: Anne Gregory

Kogan Page has joined forces with the Institute of Public Relations to publish this unique series which is designed specifically to meet the needs of the increasing numbers of people seeking to enter the public relations profession and the large band of existing PR professionals.

Taking a practical, action-orientated approach, the books in the series will concentrate on the day-to-day issues of public relations practice and management rather than academic history.

They will provide ideal primers for all those on IPR, CAM and CIM courses or those taking NVQs in PR. For PR practitioners, they will provide useful refreshers and ensure that their knowledge and skills are kept up-to-date.

Anne Gregory is Head of the School of Business Strategy and an Assistant Dean of Leeds Business School at Leeds Metropolitan University. As former Chair of the Institute of Public Relations' Education and Training Committee, Anne initiated the PR in Practice series.

Other titles in the series are:

Available from all good bookshops, or to obtain further information please contact the publishers at the address below:

Kogan Page
120 Pentonville Road, London N1 9JN
Tel: 0171 278 0433, Fax: 0171 837 6348

the Institute *of* Public Relations
PR IN PRACTICE SERIES

EFFECTIVE WRITING SKILLS FOR PUBLIC RELATIONS

John Foster

the Institute *of* Public Relations

KOGAN PAGE

YOURS TO HAVE AND TO HOLD
BUT NOT TO COPY

Kogan Page Limited
120 Pentonville Road
London N1 9JN

© John Foster, 1998

The right of John Foster to be identified as the author of this work has been asserted by him in accordance with the Copyright, Designs and Patents Act 1988.

British Library Cataloguing in Publication Data
A CIP record for this book is available from the British Library.

ISBN 0 7494 2643 8

Typeset by BookEns Ltd, Royston, Herts.
Printed and bound in Great Britain by Biddles Ltd, Guildford and Kings Lynn.

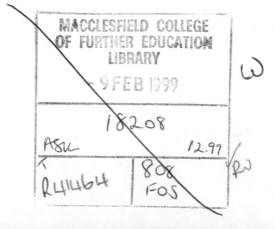

Contents

The Institute of Public Relations (IPR)

The IPR is the professional body for public relations in the UK. Its role is:
- to provide a professional structure for the practice of public relations;
- to enhance the ability and status of its members as professional practitioners;
- to represent the interests of its members;
- to provide opportunities for members to meet and exchange views and ideas;
- to offer a range of services of professional and personal benefit to members.

Founded in 1948, the Institute now has over 5,400 members practising in consultancies and in-house in all sectors of the UK economy. Members, whether generalist or specialist, are drawn from all areas of practice and management, up to main Board level, in industry and commerce, local and central government, in health and education services and charities, in the police and armed forces, in privatized and nationally owned utilities and services.

Membership of the Institute of Public Relations

Since January 1992 full membership (MIPR) of the Institute has been gained only by qualification combined with a period of professional experience, although for senior practitioners the qualification element may be substituted by ten years' experience. The criteria established for the qualification element is to reach, both in range and depth, the standards laid down in the Public Relations Education and Training Matrix.

One consequence of this decision is that, increasingly over time, membership will comprise practitioners and managers who have a formally recognized public relations qualification.

The Institute also offers Student membership and Associate membership (AMIPR) for those on their way to full membership. Affiliate membership is for those who work in a specialized area of communication and who support the Institute's aims, but who would not be entitled to full membership. Fellowship (FIPR) is awarded to Members in recognition of outstanding work in public relations.

For further information please contact:

The Institute of Public Relations
The Old Trading House
15 Northburgh Street
London EC1V 0PR
Tel: 0171 253 5151
Fax: 0171 490 0588

About the author

John Foster spent several years in journalism with weekly trade papers, finally as assistant editor of a leading printing industry magazine and as editor of a quarterly journal on platemaking for print production.

He subsequently held public relations posts with Pira International, the technology centre for the printing, paper, packaging and publishing industries, and with the Institute of Practitioners in Advertising (IPA) which represents the interests of UK advertising agencies.

He has written, edited and produced a variety of printwork, from house journals and books to posters, brochures and leaflets plus writing news releases, speeches, film scripts, slide presentations and exhibition panels. For the past six years, as a specialist freelance journalist, he has written on management and technical issues in the printing industry. He has also undertaken public relations projects in the field of healthcare.

A keen advocate of good, consistent style in the written and spoken word, John Foster has contributed the 'Verbals' column in the *IPR Journal* since 1993. He is a Fellow of the IPR and holds the CAM Diploma in Public Relations. A member of the Institute since 1954, he has served on the Council, Board of Management and Membership Committee, and was Programme Director from 1979–81. He is an honorary member of the IPA, a member of the CAM Education Foundation and an associate member of the Foreign Press Association.

Acknowledgements

I wish to thank the many friends and colleagues who helped in the preparation of this book. In particular, grateful appreciation is recorded to Nigel Ellis, former IPR president, who read the early drafts of every chapter and made many helpful suggestions for improvements.

Special thanks are also due to Pat Bowman, former head of PR at Lloyds Bank, to Don Billet, former public affairs director, Du Pont de Nemours International, to Robin Paterson, formerly senior public affairs specialist, DuPont (UK) and to Peter C Jackson, editor and communications consultant, all of whom read individual chapters or sections and made helpful comments and alterations to the original text. Feona McEwan, communications director of WPP Group PLC and Marion Clarke, corporate communications manager of Pira International, provided much useful additional information. Barry Arnold, managing director, F S Moore Ltd, printers, gave permission to reproduce typefaces in chapters six and seven.

Grateful acknowledgement must go to Anne Gregory, assistant dean of the Business School, Leeds Metropolitan University and editor of this series of IPR textbooks, for her constant support and encouragement and for letting me get on with it as I wished.

I have referred to several titles published by Oxford University Press in the preparation of this work and thank them for permission to quote information, references and examples from *Fowler's Modern English Usage, The Oxford Guide to English Usage, The Oxford Dictionary of Grammar*, and *Hart's Rules for Compositors and Readers*. Acknowledgement is also given to Headline Book Publishing Ltd for permission to quote examples from *Debrett's Correct Form*.

Foreword

Writing good English must be one of the most difficult jobs in the world. The tracking of a developing language that is rich, diverse and constantly evolving in use and meaning is not an easy task. Today's rules and uses quickly become outdated, but this book captures English as it should be used now.

There have always been books on grammar and most of us , if we are honest, have to sneak the occasional look to check whether an apostrophe is in the right place or where a quote mark goes.

This book by John Foster gives invaluable advice, not only on the rules of English grammar, but on how to make the language come alive. How do you make people excited by your writing style and keep them reading on? How do you delight and surprise them, even if the topic is essentially dull?

Of course there's writing and there's writing. Writing for the press is very different from writing for the office. John takes us through the basics of style for all occasions, right down to pronunciation.

Also included, are two very useful appendices: one on definitions of grammar with good practical examples and the other on similar pairs of words that are often confused.

The book is written in a lively, imaginitive style and is suited not only for the new practitioner who is eager to improve their mastery of the English language, but for the more experienced practitioner who needs a quick checklist of the essentials of grammar and some hints on how to pep-up their writing style.

Effective Writing Skills for Public Relations is intended to be a no-nonsense guide for busy practitioners. It avoids the traps of being so comprehensive and detailed that it confuses, or so superficial as to be of no use at all. It covers all the major grammatical constructions that we use day-to-day with the one objective in mind: writing good readable English. Every PR practitioner should have one.

Anne Gregory
Series Editor

Introduction

Style is the crucial ingredient for everything we say and do: in writing, it is the way sentences are structured, the choice of words and the way they are used, plus punctuation. If the style is outmoded and all over the place, the reader will soon lose interest and might not even get beyond the first few lines. Style calls for clarity, brevity coupled with the use of plain language, and the avoidance of clichés and jargon. It means making sure spellings are correct and that words are not misused. Above all it means consistency.

This book has been designed for students and others entering the communications industry, in particular those intending to follow a career in public relations. It will also be helpful for those already employed in the public relations profession either in consultancies or as in-house practitioners – in fact for anyone earning their living by their writing skills.

The advice in these pages is based on the authority of established style guides, in particular the *Oxford Guide to English Usage* and *Hart's Rules for Compositors and Readers*, and also on personal experience. This has covered many years of close involvement in writing, editing and producing publications of many kinds; from technical and scientific material to professional and trade journals, news releases, and general printwork including booklets, brochures, manuals and leaflets.

Effective Writing Skills deals not only with the printed but also the spoken word: for messages to be properly communicated and understood, clarity of speech is essential and a chapter is included for those giving audio-visual presentations and taking on public-speaking assignments.

While readers will benefit from reading this book from cover to cover, some will doubtless wish to dip into individual chapters as needs dictate. If some sections, such as the positioning of apostrophes, appear to be elementary, there will always be someone not far away who is getting it wrong!

This is not a book of grammar, but does serve as a reminder of some of the basic principles. The emphasis throughout is on those style points which are frequent causes of argument and disagreement: for example when and where to put capitals, how to deal with figures and abbreviations, plus the editing skills such as hyphenating, punctuating and paragraphing.

Other chapters cover the essential requirements for handling headlines and captions, as well as the basics of news releases and the need for concise language coupled with the readability of the printed word. These and other chapters will provide practitioners with a useful reference source for their day-to-day work.

Every organization should have a house style, and that very often calls for a 'style policeman' to make sure that the rules are followed by everyone, from director and manager to all support staff. If that is achieved, and if as a result there is closer interest and awareness of style, then this book will have met its objective.

1

The importance of style: an overview

Effective communication demands clear, consistent style. Everyone in public relations – whether in-house or a consultancy practitioner – should put style at the top of their priority list. This book is about the various characteristics of the written and spoken word, or the manner of writing and speaking; in other words the style, the ultimate hallmark of professionalism. It is not about English grammar, although it touches upon some of the hotly argued rules that tend to be the territory of the pedant. The basic terminology of grammar is explained in Appendix 1 to enable the reader to check up on the technicalities and to provide a refresher if needed.

The following chapters enlarge upon the topics discussed by the 'Verbals' column in the *IPR Journal* which has been running since 1993. The interest generated by these articles led me to embark upon this work which, it is hoped, will lead to a greater awareness of the importance of style. First, pay close attention to what newspapers and magazines do, and also to developments in book publishing. As soon as a new book comes out on style and usage, get a copy and start a collection. This will be invaluable when you want to establish a set of house rules, to update an existing one, or just for day-to-day reference.

Style on the move

Style changes fast. Compare, for instance, a magazine or newspaper printed only a few decades ago with one of the 1990s: over-use of capitals, stilted phraseology and solid slabs of type unrelieved by subheadings were all commonplace in the 1950s and 1960s. Even now, it is not hard to find press releases ridden with banalities, boring headlines, 'label' headings devoid of verb and verve, poorly punctuated reports and letters; and, probably worst of all, inconsistencies in spelling (let alone howlers like 'one *foul* swoop' from a BBC newscaster early in 1997).

The ignorance which surrounds modern style trends emanates through lack of interest in the subject. For young people entering the competitive world of communications it is essential to have a grasp of the basics: to know, for instance, that *media* and *data* are plural nouns, to understand the difference between a colon and a semi-colon, to appreciate that a dash and a hyphen are not the same thing. (It was this last point, incidentally, which led to the first 'Verbals' column in the *IPR Journal*.)

Some will no doubt wonder what all the fuss is about. But the hyphen masquerading as a dash is symptomatic of the lax attitude towards style; few secretaries and word-processor operators bother whether style is consistent, or even know what it means. So it is up to the public relations executive – in fact all professional communicators – to get the message across that style matters in everything an organization does.

Appreciating style

Acquiring a grounding in grammar is not enough: the finer points of style and presentation will often make all the difference between a good and a mediocre publication – between a stodgy leaflet or complex, wordy brochure and one which is lively and appealing. This means printwork that promotes a product or service and turns a glancer into a reader; that tells a story succinctly and in plain language; and is consistent in every respect. If this is achieved then the style has worked, communication has done its job and the public relations effort has paid off.

It is essential for everyone in PR and communications to have an appreciation of style so that the reader, or receiver of the message, is on the side of the sender from the outset. Just as important is visual presentation style: well-crafted slides where the logo is always the same size and colour, and text mirroring the typeface, are but two essential requirements for a corporate identity – the hallmark of a successful and profitable company or organization.

Packs and display panels with a recognizable type style are instantly identified with the company and product. If that happens, the PR effort has worked and produced tangible results. Clear, unambiguous, concise copy written in a newsy way is usually the best means of getting your message across and making it work for you, your company or your client. There are other times, however, when a more measured style is appropriate – much depends on the target audience and the marketing objectives.

Your organization's style

Style extends beyond the confines of print presentations and the printed word in packaging. It applies to the livery for your delivery van or lorry; to news releases; to film; to audio-visuals; to how your story is put over in speeches at conferences and seminars; to product labelling and design; to office stationery; and even to the way your receptionist answers the telephone. Stick to the style you have adopted in absolutely everything concerning your company or your client's products and services.

Think about it in all the tasks you perform. Is it consistent? is it doing justice to your endeavours? Is it, in fact, good PR?

There are a number of style guides to assist you and some of the best known are mentioned in later chapters. They deal mainly with the printed word, for that is where style is most important and where guidance is often needed. As journalists are inculcated with a sense of style from the moment they join a newspaper or magazine, it is helpful to see how newspapers and magazines treat the printed word. Most newspapers produce style guides for their editorial staff and it is worthwhile asking for copies.

There is, for instance, wide variation between one newspaper or magazine and another in the use of titles, the way dates are set out, and how abbreviations are handled. When writing articles for the press you should preferably type the copy in the publication's style, so check on the way figures are set; how names are written; when and where capitals are used; how quotes are dealt with; whether copy is set ragged right or justified with both edges aligned; whether -*ise* or -*ize* endings are used. A public relations executive who writes material specifically for a target media and follows its style has a far better chance of getting material published than one who ignores it.

Press releases should follow the general style adopted by newspapers for the treatment of quotations, for example double quote marks rather than single, with short sentences and paragraphs. If points like these are all followed then the sub-editor will be on the writer's side, and your copy is less likely to be changed. A bonus for the public relations executive if the chairman's favourite phrase remains unaltered!

Keep it consistent

Yet there is nothing sacrosanct about style: it is constantly changing, with spellings, 'vogue' words and phrases falling into disuse, to be replaced smartly by new ones. Favourite sayings become clichés, and the myths that infinitives must not be split, that sentences must never end with a preposition, and that words that once were capitalized can now be lower-cased with abandon, are now mainly discarded.

On the other hand, some style rules like never starting a sentence with a figure, or numbers up to and including ten always being spelt out unless they are part of a table or figure are still firmly established in style books. But whatever you decide on, you need to keep it consistent throughout the whole piece.

Avoid these

Be on your guard against repetition, or using the wrong word and putting your reader off for good. Perhaps it won't be noticed, but mostly it will. *Imply* is not the same as *infer*; there are no degrees of uniqueness (something is either unique or it isn't); *fewer than* is often used for *less than* and vice versa (*fewer* is not interchangeable with *less*); and so on. Keep it simple and understandable: use short rather than long words, write snappy sentences, cut out jargon and over-worked words, and leave foreign words to the specialist journal. But don't hesitate, occasionally, to launch into 'Franglais' (*le Channel Tunnel*) or German-English (*Die Teenagers*) or even *ein steadyseller* (for the bookshop) to provide a breather and a spot of humour.

Usage differs enormously: English is spoken by over 300 million people throughout the world, while several million more speak it as a second language. Writers have at their command more than half a million words (there are some 600,000 in the latest edition of the *Oxford English Dictionary* (*OED*)), yet it has been estimated that most people go through life with only some 2000 words at their command. This limit on the average person's vocabulary shows there is good reason for avoiding long or little-used words: not only do they fail to communicate, but the writer is felt to 'talk down' to the reader.

A number of rules for style and usage have been proposed by journalists, lexicographers and others, but few are set in stone;

the advice and examples given in this book are based on current best practice, although allowance must be made for individual taste. English is a living language always on the move: today's style will soon be yesterday's.

The guidance in these pages will help public relations practitioners and other communicators to lay down effective style rules for their own companies and organizations. Once these have been established, they should be rigorously followed. If they are not, then style becomes inconsistent and that is almost as bad as not having any rules at all. All the work that has gone into establishing the style will be wasted. But not for long: it will be revision time again before you know it!

Good style is good manners

Good style means good work. It also means good manners: letters being answered promptly, returning telephone calls, sincerity in everything you say and do. If you cannot do something, say so – don't just leave it and hope that the problem will go away. And when Christmas comes, don't send out an unsigned card, even if your company's name and address is printed inside.

Style is just as important with the spoken word. Few speakers at a conference would think of muttering and mumbling their way through a talk. Carefully enunciated speech without clichés or jargon is essential for avoiding slipshod presentation and ensuring effective communication. Some hints and tips on pronunciation style will be found in the final chapter. And as Trevor McDonald, the ITN newscaster and leader of the Campaign for Better English confirms, well-articulated speech can raise someone from humble origins to the very top. McDonald advises young people aiming for wider horizons to speak their language well. Diction and grammar really do matter.

Appreciate the need for style, be aware of style, and follow it through relentlessly and consistently. This book will help you to do that.

2

Trouble with plurals and possessives

How many times have you seen attempts to make words ending in -ey into plurals just by adding an 's' and ending up with *daiseys*? Or even worse – *tomato's*, a familiar notice in the high street? Errors like these would be immediately spotted by professional communicators, and staff in PR departments making them would not last for long. But there are plenty of difficult plurals and it is not always easy to tell from the office dictionary how to deal with them. Similarly, there is often confusion about how to handle possessives: not just to know whether an apostrophe should be there, but where to place it. Again, how frequently have you seen the possessive *its* with an apostrophe shouting at you, pretending that *it's* is OK?

Plural matters

Common problems

Most nouns require an 's' to make them plural. Because of the needs of pronunciation, with some words it is necessary to put in an 'e' to give an extra vowel (*branches*), with different rules for changing vowel sounds (*stomachs*). Particular difficulty is encountered with words ending in -o: *embargoes* but *mementos*. A useful rule here is that -e is never inserted when another vowel comes before -o: an instant answer to any thought of putting an 'e' in *ratios*. Note that there are *roofs*, not rooves; *wharves* but *dwarfs*; *scarves* but *turfs*.

Compound words made up of a noun and adjective, or two nouns connected by a preposition form plurals by a change in the main word as in *courts martial, heirs presumptive, poets laureate* and in *sons-in-law, hangers-on, runners-up, passers-by* and *men-of-war*. Note, however, that there are *brigadier-generals* and *sergeant-majors*. And there are *run-throughs, set-ups* and *forget-me-nots, handfuls* and *spoonfuls*.

Care is needed with plurals for words of foreign origin and it must be noted here that *media/data* are plural nouns and take a plural verb. However, the new edition of *Fowler's Modern English Usage* says 'we are "still at the debating table" on the question of *the media is/are*', but nevertheless recommends the use of the plural when in doubt. (In informal writing, or speech, only the purist will object to *the media is/data is*.) Misuse of *criteria* and *phenomena* is common as they are mistaken for being collective, singular nouns: the singular forms are *criterion* and *phenomenon*. It should be noted that *graffiti* is the plural of *graffito, termini* of *terminus, viruses* of *virus* and *bacteria* of *bacterium*.

Some other plurals: *analyses, appendices, basis/es, bureaux* (but often Anglicized to *bureaus*), *indexes* (but *indices* in mathematics), *memorandums* (but *memoranda* in a collective sense), *moratoriums, referendums, quorums* (but *addenda, curricula*), *stadiums* (try saying *stadia/syllabi* and you are in danger of being pedantic and bowing to the purist); also *synopses, syllabuses, theses*. An extensive list of foreign words in their singular and plural forms will be found in *Hart's Rules*.

Singular or plural for collective nouns?

There is a problem for the writer using a collective noun: should it take a singular or plural verb? The choice will depend on whether the noun is considered as a single entity or as a group of people or things. Thus, whether to write the committee *is* or *are*, *agrees* or *agree* can be answered simply by saying to yourself does it refer to the committee as a whole or to the views of separate members? Similarly, the mass noun *audience* can take either the singular or plural as in 'the audience *was* seated, ready for the speaker' or as in 'the audience *were* all clapping madly'. The same applies to other mass nouns like *board, cast* (of actors), *company, family, group, government, staff.*

It is important to decide if the emphasis lies on the individual or the group with a word like *board*, to take one example. If it lies on the individual members of the board, then write the board '*who* broke off for lunch' but if the sense is collective, the construction would be 'the board *which* made a decision'. The singular always follows if the noun has a qualifier like *this, that, every* as in 'every manager has a part to play'.

As a general rule, it is better to have a singular verb with a collective noun, and to treat names of companies and organizations as singular entities. The plural form tends to smack of informality: 'XYZ company *are announcing*' is a relaxed and friendly style, but loses crispness. In the end, however, house style will decide – another reason for every company to have a set of rules for basic style points such as this.

Whether to write *is* or *are* for companies with more than one name, such as Legal & General, is somewhat of a conundrum, and one faced sooner or later by everyone. While it is largely a matter of house style, Marks & Spencer and the multi-name styles for PR consultancies and advertising agencies mostly take the singular verb, thus adhering to the general rule of 'keep it singular'.

Note, however, that *a pair* and *a couple* take the plural, as do two singular nouns linked by *and* unless the conjoined words form a single idea as in *wining and dining*. Conversely, note that the number *is*, public relations *is*. Other nouns taking a singular verb include *advice, equipment, furniture, knowledge, machinery, stationery, traffic*. There are a number of nouns which only take the plural: *people, police, clergy* and some others recognizable by their -s endings, notably *clothes, congratulations, outskirts, remains, riches, scissors, thanks*. Nouns with a plural form which do take a singular verb are *billiards, measles, news*.

The crucial point in any singular/plural dispute is to maintain consistency throughout the piece as a whole, through each sentence and each paragraph. If that consistency is lost, news releases may be rubbished, and printed documents and contact reports will mostly fail to command the reader's respect.

Communication or communications?

Difficulty also arises in distinguishing between the terms communication and communications. Even public relations practitioners have a problem with this and argument rages: both refer to the act of communicating, the latter relating to the technicalities or the hardware of communicating – e-mail, faxes, telephones and so on. Confusion is compounded by the fact that there are courses in *communication* management, and that *communications* can be managed. In reality, there is little difference in meaning. So, take your pick!

It is relevant to note that the titles communications manager/ consultant have largely replaced the title public relations officer which has now become somewhat outdated. But whatever the title – whether for undertaking the mechanics of communications or for advising how a company communicates with its public – the context will usually clarify job descriptions. Again, consistency is the watchword.

Apostrophe problems

Trouble with possessives

It seems that knowing where to put the apostrophe in

possessives – indicating possession or ownership – causes as much difficulty as any other mark. Kingsley Amis in *The King's English* says that if it hasn't been mastered by the age of 14 then the chances are that there will always be the possibility of error. There is often confusion between *its* (in the possessive) and *it's*, the shortened form of *it is*. And the apostrophe is further misused when denoting the plural – the so-called greengrocer's apostrophe as in *potato's* (or perhaps even *potatoe's*!) – or when letter(s) have been omitted.

First, take the basic rules for positioning the apostrophe for a possessive. When the thing or person is in the singular then the apostrophe goes before the 's' as in the *boy's tie*. If, however, there is more than one boy, the apostrophe goes after the 's' as in the *boys' ties*. Another example: in *the cat's paws* there is one cat and as the paws belong to the cat it is the cat that is in the possessive, and since it is one cat the apostrophe goes before the 's'. You talk about *the campaign's objective* (where there is one campaign and one or more objectives); *John's brother* (or *brothers*, it doesn't matter) there is one John and the name is in the singular. When there are several journalists, you talk about *journalists' needs*.

For singular words ending in 's', just add 's as in the *boss's office*. To form the plural possessive, add 'e' apostrophe after the 's' as in *the bosses' bonus, the Joneses' dog*. With plural words that end with an 's', simply add the apostrophe as in the *ladies' room*, the *Smiths' house*. For nouns that are already plural as in *children, men, women* add an apostrophe 's' in the same way: *children's, men's, women's, people's*. Never write *childrens', mens', womens'* or *peoples'* or leave out the apostrophe altogether, even though you might be tempted to do so.

It is quite common to see *four weeks holiday* wrongly written as a matter of course. While the clumsy *holiday of four weeks* would be pedantic in the extreme, it is far better to write *four weeks'* holiday with the apostrophe correctly positioned than not having one at all and risk offending the reader. And, of course, you go on a *fortnight's cruise*. In distinguishing the difference between *its* and *it's*, two examples will help: *its* in the possessive – the dog wagged *its* tail; *it's* as the shortened version of *it is* – the client said '*it's* a good presentation'.

Many other purposes, but don't put one if not needed

The apostrophe is a multi-purpose mark: it can signify omitted characters as in *isn't, doesn't*, and the verbal elisions *I'm, I'll, you'll, we'll*. It indicates the plural of single letters: *A's* and *B's, p's* and *q's*. Note that the apostrophe is omitted in the plurals of groups of letters and numbers as in *MPs, 1990s*, and in *whys* and *wherefores*. It would, however, be used to show an omission as in the *'90s*.

There is, of course, no apostrophe in *hers, ours, yours* or *theirs* (an apostrophe is needed in *one's*), but care is needed in distinguishing between the relative pronoun *whose* and *who's*, the shortened version of *who is*.

Leaving it out when it should be there is bad enough, but putting one in when it is not needed is worse still: not only is there the illiterate use of the apostrophe for plurals as in the greengrocers' signs for *carrot's* and *pea's* – there are now 'garage' apostrophes in advertisements for *Fiesta's* and *Mondeo's* and there are headlines for *Suzuki's* but, curiously, they advertise at the same time *Range Rovers* and *Cavaliers*, while cafés have notices for *tea's* and *coffee's*, and roadside restaurants displaying signs for *lunch's* and *dinner's*. Ouch! It happens more often than you might think.

Much of the problem comes from designers who either don't know or don't care whether there should be an apostrophe: *Grannys* (a shop), *Henrys Table* (a restaurant); but it is gratifying to see that *Sainsbury's* has stuck with tradition. And the apostrophe is often at the mercy of the designer who readily turns it into a dagger, pen or heart without a qualm, diminishing its importance and contributing if not to its demise, to uncertainty about positioning.

Inconsistencies to watch for

Organizations drop their apostrophes without hesitation, perhaps in an attempt at making them user- and customer-friendly. Thus we see *Chambers English Dictionary, Debenhams* and *Barclays Bank*; but also *Earls Court* and *St James's Square*; or *Queens' College* (Cambridge) but *Queen's College* and *All Souls* (Oxford), which all add to the inconsistencies. Some of the above can easily be checked in telephone directories, but where writers struggle is in knowing where to put the apostrophe in words ending in -s in names like Charles. *Hart's Rules* says: 'Use 's for the possessive case whenever possible.' The guidance here is that the 's should appear in all monosyllables and in longer words accented on the next to last syllable as in *Jones's, Thomas's, St James's Square*. In multi-syllable words like Nicholas, it is equally acceptable to put the apostrophe alone as in *Nicholas'* or *Nicholas's*, but if in doubt always add the 's. For *goodness' sake* always think where it should go.

It would be unwise to put *public relations* in the possessive. Try it, and the result is awful if not a tongue-twister: public relations' or public relations's are equally ugly; a better way would be to treat public relations as an adjective and so achieve, for example, the *public relations objective*, or the wordier *objective of public relations*.

While no apostrophe is needed when writing 'He will be taken to *the cleaners*,' it should appear in such constructions as 'He is going to *the butcher's*' when there is ellipsis of the word 'shop'. However, to say (or write) 'I am going to *the doctor's*' with the ellipsis of the word 'surgery' would offend many an ear or eye. In these and similar examples, it would be better to omit the 's' altogether.

There are, shown above, a number of inconsistencies in the use of the apostrophe, and it seems that incorrect usage is increasing both where the apostrophe is omitted or where it is included when it shouldn't be. The *Oxford Guide to English Usage*, as well as *Fowler's* and *Hart's Rules* should be consulted whenever in doubt. Dictionaries do not help much for dealing with these matters.

3

Making your mark

Taking care over punctuation shows that the writer has the reader in mind. Putting the correct marks – and making sure there are no unnecessary ones – aids understanding and avoids ambiguity. The comma, stop, colon and interrogation mark are not there just to satisfy the rules of construction. They have a real and active purpose: to give the reader a breather, to give a pause and, at intervals, to provide a change of pace or thought.

Too many people think that punctuation is just another chore: get on with the words, never mind the irritations of having to bother with brackets, dashes or hyphens, let alone using quote marks properly or typed the right way round. On the other hand, it is easy to over-punctuate and end up with complicated, obscure sentences and a 'spotty' page. Look now at the various marks and how they should be used and presented.

Basic punctuation

'Punctuation is made for man, not man for punctuation,'

declares *The Times Guide to English Style and Usage.* 'It is a courtesy designed to help readers to understand a story without stumbling, not a fireworks display to show off your dashes and gaspers.' That is the basic principle.

The full stop

This is the writer's best aid to crisp, clear copy. That, after all, is what the public relations practitioner should aim for when writing for the press, and indeed for most forms of communication. But that does not mean that a piece of copy should be littered with stops like currants in a pudding. A full stop (or full point to the printer) brings a sentence to an abrupt halt, ready for the next one and an expansion of thought. No stop is needed when ending a sentence with a question mark, exclamation mark or if ending a sentence with a quotation which itself ends with a full stop.

But there are other uses: for instance, a set of three is used to show an omission (use three and only three, but if they come at the end of a sentence insert a concluding one). It will soon be noticed when the incorrect number has been used – there are plenty of examples of the writer not having the faintest idea of how many stops to put and sometimes finishing up with a line of them! Full stops are rarely seen these days in sets of initials for organizations (put them between the initials IPR and it will immediately look old-fashioned).

Stops are fast disappearing from initials of company names, but they can be used with great effect and impact in advertisement display heads. They should not appear in headings for press release stories for the simple reason that they are hardly ever seen in newspaper or magazine headlines. Do not put them after abbreviations like Mr, Mrs, Ms, or in lb, in, ft, unless of course they come at the end of a sentence.

The comma

This is one of the most common marks, but often misused: either it is put in when not needed or it is in the wrong place.

Typically, the comma is used to encase a job title or descriptive phrase after a name. But a very usual mistake is just to put an opening comma, leaving the rest of the description dangling and yelling out for a companion comma.

The comma separates adjectives qualifying a noun as in *small, profitable consultancy* but there is no comma when one adjective qualifies another, for example *a bright red tie*. They are useful for breaking up a long sentence, but take care not to put in too many and cause greater confusion than having none at all.

Some dos and don'ts. A comma would only go before *and* in a list of items if one of those items includes another *and*. Do not put commas in dates or round adverbs and adverbial phrases unless special emphasis is required. They do not normally go before or after *therefore* and *accordingly*, but they always encase *however* when there is a change of thought. And do not, at least in copy for press or printwork, put a comma before a direct quote – a colon should be used here.

The colon

This is a useful mark for the writer of news releases, and copy for articles and house journals. It is normal journalistic practice to use a colon to introduce a quote as in Joe Bloggs said: 'This is the best way of doing it.' (Teachers and college instructors, who seldom have any knowledge of, or interest in, typography, usually insist upon a comma before the quote – perhaps this is why this style is seen so often.) The colon is useful for starting a list, but do not put a dash after it as in :— where the dash is superfluous. It is also handy for leading the reader to fresh fact or thought or to follow the expressions *such as, for example, namely, the following*.

The semicolon

This little-used mark deserves greater awareness of its attributes. While in no sense a substitute for the comma, the semicolon provides a far stronger break and a longer pause, and it can perform some of the comma's functions. It can separate two or more clauses of equal importance and is useful for listing words and phrases that cannot neatly be separated by commas. In a lengthy sentence, it can bring a thought to a halt, enabling a new one to be started, so aiding clarity. Some writers will prefer to use a full stop instead; perhaps this is why the semicolon is falling into disuse.

Exclamation and interrogation marks

These marks normally count as a concluding full stop and take a capital letter afterwards. But they are sometimes seen after a supporting clause in brackets within a sentence. The interrogation (question) mark never follows indirect speech, or statements that pose a question; only direct questions – as used in quotes.

Brackets, round and square

When using round brackets to enclose a complete sentence, put the full stop *inside* the closing bracket as in (*This is the way to do it.*). It goes *outside* only if the last part of the sentence is in brackets. The square bracket is used to denote comments or explanations added to the original text, usually by the editor or someone other than the author.

The dash

This is used to add an afterthought or, if used as a pair, to replace commas if there are already too many in the sentence. Many writers are getting into the habit of using a hyphen instead of a dash: this on the face of it seems to matter little, but there is a distinct difference between the two marks: the dash (known to the printer as the en-dash) is twice as long as the hyphen and when they are both used in the same piece – as very often happens – something is clearly amiss. The hyphen masquerading as the dash is a common fault, but seldom seen in newspapers and magazines and in well-designed house journals and printwork.

Unlike the manual typewriter, today's keyboards do not

usually have a dash key and that is how the trouble starts. To print a dash with a word processor or computer, at least two keys are usually needed and reference should be made to the operating manual or to the software supplier for advice on achieving a proper en-dash. A final word: journalists on *The Times* are advised to avoid dashes which, says their style guide, 'often indicate that a sentence is badly constructed and needs rewriting'. Other newspapers take a more relaxed stance and there can be no arbiter of style points such as this. If dashes are employed, they must be used sparingly and certainly only once in a paragraph.

The hyphen

Hyphens indicate when two or more words should be read together and taken as one. A check with the dictionary will quickly tell whether a word is hyphenated or not. They will enable the reader to distinguish between, for example, *recover* (from an illness) and re-cover (with material). Modern style soon overturns established practice, and words that were once hyphenated are now seen as one: *payphone, feedback, multinationals, wildlife* for instance. Few in PR would think of writing *lay-out* or *hand-out*!

Once a hyphenated word assumes everyday usage, it is not long before the hyphen disappears. The closed up form usually looks and 'feels' better; a hyphen in the middle looks a touch pedantic and ugly to some eyes. Hyphens are happiest when used in numbers (*twenty-one*) or as fractions (*two-thirds*). And they are useful for separating similar vowel sounds (*co-ordinate/co-operate* for instance). The main purpose of a hyphen is to avoid ambiguity as in *five-year-old children*. But always ensure that if you do use a hyphen it has a job to do. Whether or not to hyphenate is hardly a subject of breathtaking importance. Study current style and decide for yourself.

The apostrophe

The main use of the apostrophe is to denote the possessive case, a subject discussed at length in the previous chapter (see page 26). It is also used as a mark of omission: it can signify omitted characters as in *isn't, doesn't, I'm*; it distinguishes between *its* and *it's*; it indicates the plural of single letters, A's and B's.

When you are quoting...

Quotation marks often give trouble. The writer who knows that a word or phrase is not the right one gets over the problem by enclosing it in quotes; at other times, there may not be a need for quote marks at all. Further, there is often uncertainty about whether to use single or double quotes, and on the placing of punctuation within them. Consider now some of the pitfalls.

Try not to use them for facetious, technical or slang words. Their proper, and most usual place, is for direct speech quotations: hence the term quotes or quote marks. (The phrase 'inverted commas' is old-fashioned and not the way journalists would describe them.) They should be used for words or phrases not yet in everyday use – but only sparingly. Include them for titles of articles in magazines or chapters of books, but again avoid over-use. Do not use them for house names as there is no logic or merit for doing so.

Single or double?

Most publishers nowadays use the single quote mark for direct quotations, inserting the double mark for quotes within a quote. This does not, however, apply to newspapers whose editors will favour double quotes for quoted speech and for the single mark for quotes within. Consequently, the double quote style should be used for press releases and news-type publications. For example, a chairman's address to an AGM might contain a quote from the marketing director; in which case the release would be typed with double quotes for the main statement and with single quotes for the marketing director's comments inside it.

Misuse occurs when there are several paragraphs of quoted speech. Quotes get closed at the end of each paragraph and opened again at the next paragraph. But the opening quote marks should go at the beginning of each paragraph and only appear at the *end* of the quote. If the text reverts to reported speech at any point the quote should be closed, and only opened again when direct speech restarts.

As a general rule, punctuation marks go *inside* the quote marks (single or double as style dictates) when they refer to the words quoted, as in the managing director said: 'When will dividends be sent out?' but *outside* if they are part of a longer sentence carrying the quotation: the chairman commented on the company's 'excellent year'. If the complete sentence is a quotation the final point goes *inside*, as follows: 'The marketing director wants greater effort by the sales staff.'

Students of style will find guidance on the relative placing of punctuation and quotation marks in most style books, with *Hart's Rules* giving detailed advice and a variety of examples. And take a look to see how newspapers deal with this point; they provide an excellent guide to the treatment of quotations, and they are at your elbow every day.

Unless the piece contains a number of direct quotes, general guidance gives that quotation marks be used sparingly. You can often avoid them altogether by indenting the paragraph (or paragraphs) and setting the type in a smaller size. Take special care when using direct quotes: make sure they are verbatim. The last thing you want is the person to whom the quote was attributed later denying the words were ever said! And it goes without saying that the writer must be sure the quoted words were not in any way defamatory.

Finally, when proofreading, ensure that the quote marks are the right way round. They are easy to spot and you will surprise yourself when you see how many word processor operators get them wrong. They can be corrected easily by typing the key twice and then deleting the unwanted one. The pity is that so many typists cannot be bothered to do that. But they usually remember that a capital letter follows all punctuation marks except a comma, colon, semicolon and quote marks within a sentence. When and when not to use capitals will be the subject of the next chapter.

4

Down with capitalism!

Only journalists and those committed to style principles appear to know or care where or when initial capital letters should be used. Whether to capitalize a word or not is one of the most hotly argued points in any office, particularly when preparing copy for publication. The only rule that most people can remember is: capital letter for the particular, small for the general. That is all right as far as it goes, but where is the dividing line? Is there too much capitalization anyway? What, if any, are the guidelines?

Consistency is the essence

Dictionaries are helpful when you are uncertain whether to capitalize, and they should be consulted before reaching for the style guide or entering into a heated discussion. Uncertainty exists over words that have dual meanings. For example, a few years ago it was fashionable to give the word 'press', when referring to the media, a capital 'p'. Current style now demands a small 'p' which is logical since context will always make the meaning clear.

Consistency is of paramount importance. Nothing looks worse than a publication displaying irregular capitalization; this looks haphazard. If the name of a firm's department is used first with a capital letter and soon after with a small initial letter, the reader is immediately confused. On top of that it looks as though an amateur has been at work. If you are unsure whether to use a capital, it is better to retain consistency rather than risk style absurdities with some words of similar meaning given a capital and others not.

Always aim to keep capitals to a minimum. Too many spoil the appearance of the page, look old-fashioned and fail to follow modern style. Imagine a line of type with the 'up and down' look; the eye is quickly distracted, making reading difficult. Such was the style of many of the books and magazines published up to the 1950s. Compare today's style, and the difference is staggering: a continuous flow of small characters is easy on the eye and modern-looking.

Problem words, particularly when it comes to preparing copy for desktop publishing, are those which sometimes take an initial capital and other times do not. It is important for every organization to have firm rules for the capitalization of commonly used words. The fewer the capitals, the easier it is to be consistent and the better looking the printed page. In short, down with the capitalists!

Why lower case, upper case?

Another way to describe capitals is to call them 'upper case' and small letters 'lower case'. These terms are now universally accepted and derive from the time when printers' compositors kept their small type characters in low cases, close to hand, while those characters in less frequent use were stored in a higher (upper) case. Thus, if a line of type is set with a mixture of small and capital letters it is said by the printer to be in 'upper and lower case' and marked u&lc, as opposed to text set completely in capitals, or very rarely in lower case only (a style for just a few words for display purposes for example).

When to use capitals

A capital is used for the first word in every sentence. It follows a full stop, question and interrogation marks, is used at the opening of a quote if it begins a sentence, and also for months and days of the week. Capitals should be used for proper nouns or names (words referring to a particular person or place), for formal titles, names of companies and organizations, political parties, titles of newspapers and magazines, titles of newspaper and periodical articles, books, films, trade names, names of ships and aircraft types. They are usually used for abbreviations, although some organizations adopt a lower case style in order to reflect advertising or product branding.

Where difficulties occur

Job titles

This is where a lot of difficulty arises. The advice here is to follow newspaper style which generally uses lower case where the title is descriptive as in managing director, marketing director or communications manager. Some will no doubt find it hard to accept a lower case style for job titles, but once used to it the small letters look right and objections diminish. It is seen often enough in the press.

For titles that are both formal and descriptive, such as President, use capitals for a full reference, as in John Smith, President of XYZ Association. Subsequent mentions could just be John Smith, the president. The same applies to royalty: Prince Charles becomes 'the prince' and the Princess Royal 'the princess' in subsequent references. Further examples will be found in *Hart's Rules*, which notes that 'monarch' and 'sovereign' can be set lower case if used in a general sense.

Capitals for a company?

Stockbrokers, thankfully, no longer refer to their partnerships as 'the Firm'. Nevertheless, many executives insist upon using a capital initial letter for 'company' in the mistaken belief that the capital somehow bestows importance. The only time for a capital is when the name of the firm or company is spelt out in full.

The government

When writing about the government, always use lower case unless you are making a formal reference to Her Majesty's Government. Acts only carry upper case when their full titles are used; the same applies to bills and white papers. Use lower case for the ministry and minister, but capitals when putting the title in full. Note that if the office holder is referred to only by their office, the titles prime minister, chancellor of the exchequer, foreign secretary and so on are in lower case in some national newspapers. Most will use capitals when the complete name and formal title are given. Use upper and lower case for the House of Commons, House of Lords, Department of Trade and Industry; but the department or DTI in subsequent references. Put left/right (wing), the speaker, the opposition, the cabinet.

When referring to political parties, the name of the party should be in upper case as in 'the Labour Party', while retaining the capital for general references when the word 'party' is not used. However, when used as a normal adjective, write lower case as in conservative outlook, socialist objectives. Members of Parliament are capitalized to MPs, not MP's, and certainly not MsP.

The seasons

Some writers feel that somehow the seasons are so important that they must be capitalized. This is nonsense and is not supported by style guides. But note that religious festivals such as Easter take capitals. So does Christmas, but new year or new year's day need not.

Geographical regions

Recognizable regions such as Northern Ireland carry capitals, but are lower case if referring to northern England for example. Capitals are well established for the North-East, the North and the West Country, but here again it would scarcely cause offence if these regions lost their capital letters.

Derivatives

Adjectives derived from proper names carry capitals, for example; Christian, Catholic. But note that you wear wellingtons (hence *wellies*) and a jersey; and that we have amperes and volts. Use lower case when connection with the proper name is remote, as in arabic (letters), french (chalk, polish, windows), italic (script), roman (numerals). Use lower case for gargantuan and herculean, but with less familiar words use a capital, as in Draconian.

Trade names

All registered trade names must carry a capital letter. A frequent error is to give a lower case 's' to Sellotape, an 'h' for Hoover, a 'k' for Kodak. Note capitals for Filofax, Marmite, Pyrex, Vaseline, Xerox. To find out whether a word is, in fact, a trade name and needs a capital, check with the *Kompass Register of Industrial Trade Names*, available in public reference libraries, or with the Register of Trade Names held at the Patent Office in London, Newport and Manchester.

Committees

Names of committees, particularly those of an official nature, should be in capitals. Style will vary from one organization to another, but so long as the writer is consistent and follows house style, there can be little argument.

The trend is to knock it down

The above examples are included to show the narrow divide between choice of capital or small letter. Style is constantly changing and words that were once always capitalized will soon be lower-cased. Even if you don't notice the 'knock it down' trend, and still want to use capitals when no one else does, do use lower case until to do so would look stupid and out of place. The general rule is to capitalize titles of organizations, not those of people.

Do not use capitals for words one after the other in a line. This is often done in the belief that a fully capitalized line will have added emphasis and the reader will take more notice of it. While a few capitalized words might stand out, too many or a line-full will be self-defeating: they will offend the eye and not be read.

5

Clichés, jargon and other worn words

Originality of expression is the keynote to good writing style. It is the stale, worn-out phrase – the cliché – which can spoil otherwise well written and crisp copy. Likewise, jargon words which are meaningless and unintelligible fail to communicate. Avoiding clichés and jargon is not always easy. In fact there are occasions when they can be used to good effect, so long as the reader knows they are deliberate. At other times they present the only way of getting over a specific point or idea.

The word cliché (French for a duplicate printing plate, stereotype or electrotype), means a hackneyed, overworked phrase or a saying that has lost vigour and originality. In fact the word 'stereotype' is itself a cliché as it is now taken to mean a role model (also a cliché!). The difficulty for the writer is to identify such expressions and then to find others to take their places which won't turn out to be yet more clichés. Effort to express new ideas in a different way will be well rewarded. The writer will be refreshed, as will the reader.

It is important to cultivate sensitivity to the hackneyed phrase; if you can see that you have just written a cliché, this is a good sign for you can now replace it with a fresh thought. If a cliché is deliberate, or cannot be avoided, then one solution is to let the reader know you are aware of it: say so and put the word or phrase in quotes.

Catchphrases and metaphors, many of which have become firmly embedded in the English language, soon become stale if overused. Yet there can still be room for the idiomatic expression to liven up otherwise dull text – if used sparingly.

Recognizing clichés

To help you recognize tired phrases (and hopefully avoid them), here are a few in current use: *put on the back burner, bottom line, low/high profile, having said that, passed its sell-by date*; stock similes like *as hard as nails*; pompous phrases including *wind of change*, or a *sea-change development* should all get *the blue pencil* treatment. Some sayings demand instant excision: *address a problem, conventional wisdom, take on board, a wide range of issues, put on hold, state of the art, a whole new ball game, life-style, in this day and age, when it comes to the crunch, quantum leap, up front money*. These examples are only just *the tip of the iceberg*.

One of the more common expressions is *at this point in time*; this is not only a tired phrase, but tedious when a perfectly good word for the same thing is *now*. Here, it should be noted that *moment in time* is not so much a cliché as tautology since *moment* already means *point in time*. Other stock phrases to slip off the tongue or pen with ease are *at the end of the day, no Brownie points, career girl, between a rock and a hard place, now for the good/bad news*, not to mention some that have *stood the test of time* and make us *as sick as a parrot. It's as simple as that, yer know what I mean? Ah right!* Guard against what Sir Ernest Gowers in his *The Complete Plain Words* calls the 'Siamese twins' of *part and parcel*, to all *intents and purposes*, or *this day and age*.

But Gowers points out that writers would be 'needlessly

handicapped' if they were never allowed to use such phrases as *strictly speaking, rears its ugly head* or even *Hobson's choice*. Context coupled with judgement will indicate whether it is necessary to rewrite the sentence. But what is new is not necessarily better; the old saying that *there's many a good tune played on an old fiddle* still holds true today. Be on constant guard against writing clichés: when you think you are *radiantly happy* by *leaps and bounds* or want *to rule the roost*, check with Eric Partridge's *A Dictionary of Clichés*, for you will find these overused phrases listed among hundreds of other worn and tired expressions.

Business clichés are used extensively: some like *please find enclosed* are worn and faded and, thankfully disappearing. In public relations, a *client presentation, new business pitch, account win, corporate hospitality, target audience, focus group, spin doctor, methodology* (why not just *method?*) and *overkill* are stock expressions and hard to avoid. The dividing line between commonly used phrases and jargon is a fine one: both kinds are so frequently used that it is impossible to do without them.

Jargon: help or hindrance?

The word jargon was used in the late fourteenth century to mean 'the twittering of the birds' or as the latest edition of *Fowler's Modern English Usage* puts it: 'a term of contempt for something (including a foreign language) that the reader does not understand... any mode of speech abounding in unfamiliar terms... eg the specialised vocabulary of bureaucrats, scientists, or sociologists'.

Jargon is jargon when words are so technical or obscure that they defy comprehension. They contribute nothing to sense or meaning and might just as well not be written at all. Public relations and advertising jargon soon slide into the vernacular, as opposed to formal or literary English, and is used without hesitation just because everyone else speaks or writes it. That is all very well, but if it fails to communicate to those outside 'media village-speak', then there is a case for reducing it as much as possible.

There is little to choose between public relations jargon (*networking, publics, press kit/pack, coverage, perception*) and marketing idiom (*positioning, conceptual, target, focus, strategic planning*). It does not take long for jargon like this to drift into cliché and for readers quickly to tire of it: *upmarket, downsizing, downshifting, niche marketing, layered management, interface/interact, state-of-the-art* are all firmly in the language of communications. Phrases and words like *in-depth, on-going, user-friendly, cutting edge, parameters, definitive* and *conceptual* should be used sparingly or preferably avoided altogether.

Jargon is often embedded in public relations terminology. Take this example from a trade directory entry: 'Well researched communication messages, disseminated through appropriate influence channels to target professional audiences are the hallmark of an approach which...' Quite what the writer expected the reader to glean from that defies imagination.

A recent example of jargon getting out of hand is the use of *upskilling* to mean improving performance through training. Although understandable, this is jargon that is unlikely to last or ever find a place in a dictionary along with *can-do, core business, critical mass* and *eye contact*. But some jargon words can provide an element of fun and are likely to last longer, for example: *yuppie, dinkies* (double income, no kids), *woolfie* (well-off older person), *wrinkle*, along with *bimbos, foodies* and *toyboys* all of which have earned a place in the English language. Soon we are to have *mouse potatoes* (computer addicts), *netizens* and *cybernauts* (regular Internet surfers) as firm entries in the *OED*.

Apart from the specialized jargon of the legal fraternity, it is in the area of information technology where technical words are used freely in the belief that they will always be understood. For example, news releases on computer technology are notorious for being packed tight with jargon. That is acceptable for journalists from computer publications who know and understand the technical terms used, but those writing for the popular press or broadcasting will have difficulty in putting over the information and giving clear and unambiguous explanations.

Two contrasting examples of typical jargon illustrate the point: 'the stylistic expressiveness of vector based brush strokes with the speed and resolution independence of an advanced drawing application', and 'automatically generated site map using HotSauce MCF (Meta Content Format Files)'. The first assumes the reader knows exactly what is meant, but leaves room for mistake and misinterpretation, while the second makes an attempt at explanation within the body of the text, while also giving full details of the technical terms used as a footnote. If there is no alternative to a jargon word or phrase, then explain the terms in straightforward language, perhaps inserting a word or two of explanation in brackets.

Foreign words are also jargon to most readers; steer clear of them unless context demands their inclusion. Jargon baffles the reader and specialist writers should never use it for audiences outside their own field.

Catchphrases quickly become stale...

Like clichés, catchphrases quickly lose originality: the source of catchphrases is mostly the entertainment industry (films, radio and TV shows in particular), but some also come from advertising and public relations campaigns such as *It's good to talk* (BT), *For the life you don't yet know* (Allied Dunbar). These have only a limited life, but others like *virtual reality* are more likely to find a permanent place in the language. Popular catchphrases such as *mind-set, nice little earner,* or *have a nice day,* and catchwords like *loadsamoney* and other permutations of *loadsa* should be avoided since any originality has long since vanished.

It is advisable, when drafting press releases and articles in particular, to watch out for the catchphrase that might be used unwittingly and lead to editorial deletion. If catchphrases are overdone, predictability takes over and the writer is not able to take the reader by surprise and attract attention.

... so can metaphors and similes

A metaphor is a figure of speech, a way of describing an object or action imaginatively and without being directly related to it (a *glaring* error), enabling the writer to convey thoughts briefly and without having to resort to lengthy explanation. But they can easily be overworked. As Sir Ernest Gowers points out, 'sometimes they are so absurdly overtaxed that they become a laughing stock and die of ridicule'.

Avoid mixed or inappropriate metaphors, where incongruous and incompatible terms are used for the same object: *We have the key to the 21st Century* as quoted in the *Oxford Dictionary of English Grammar*. Gowers gives further explanation and examples.

A simile, also a figure of speech, compares one thing with another of a different kind and is usually identified by insertion of *as* or *like (cold as charity, deaf as a post, blush like a schoolgirl, look like grim death)*. As with metaphors, guard against overuse.

Make room for the idiom

Readers soon become bored by dull continuous text; there is always room for idiomatic expressions. Attempting to find a suitable idiomatic expression to fit the flow of thought is not easy and dictionaries are not much help. Useful collections will be found in the *Oxford Dictionary of English Idioms* which contains 7000 idioms and their variant forms plus examples in modern writing. Or there is the *Wordsworth Dictionary of Idioms* which also has several thousand examples with meanings cross-referenced by head words and first words, in three distinct categories – formal, informal and slang. Lastly there is *Chambers Idioms*, which contains several thousand entries.

In the region of (formal), *hit the headlines* (informal) and *pack it in* (slang), offer a few examples. Often defying grammatical and logical rules, idioms can give colour and vitality to a piece of writing without risking faded and overused phrases. The English language is particularly rich in idiom, but use it sparingly – slang expressions are fine in speech but should be avoided in writing.

Beware of slang

Much modern day slang owes its popularity to the advertising copywriter. Night is spelt *nite*, you is *U*, clean becomes *kleen*, flow slides to *flo*. Slang has contributed to confusion about spelling and yet despite the protestations of purists, much of it is finding its way into the language. Computer technology, multimedia, interactive television, even healthcare have all provided their own slang expressions, much of them pure jargon, intelligible only to those working in the field. Slang is for the voice, not for the pen. If you must use it, then keep it only for informal writing – the sales leaflet, correspondence or staff memos; but never for the release, the annual report or the corporate brochure.

6

Is it easy to read?

The words are as you want them, you have got rid of clichés and jargon, the punctuation is right – in fact the style so far is just about spot on. But there is more to it than that. No matter how much effort has been put into the text, it will be wasted if it is hard to read. Readability is a complex subject and is the province of the designer and typographer. There are, nevertheless, some basic principles to be considered now that desktop publishing (DTP) is so widely used. And when the disk goes off to the printers for a publication or document you want to be sure that when the proof comes back it will be right both textually and visually.

Even if the work is going to an outside consultancy before printing, the copy must be prepared in such a way that the presentation style will be followed at the final stages of typographical design. For internal documents, too, care must be taken to see that the visual style is going to help the reader – in short, be easy on the eye. For if it isn't then there is an instant barrier to communication.

This section covers important factors in readability and concentrates on the overall appearance, whether you have a straightforward word-processed document or a print job from

DTP origination. The pros and cons of one design against another will not be considered here, nor will guidance be offered on how printwork should be designed, as these are subjective and beyond the scope of this book.

Edit with the reader in mind

Always consider the appearance of the page when editing. Avoid the 'grey' look which results when slabs of type matter are unrelieved by paragraph breaks or subsidiary headings and illustrations. Depending on the subject matter, make headings as lively as possible so that they not only drive the text forwards but make the page look attractive to the eye.

One sure way of achieving interest is to start the text with a drop initial letter, usually larger and bolder than the rest of the copy. This can increase readership by as much as ten per cent. Some designers specify fancy and seldom-used typefaces for the drop initial letter, but these are usually unnecessary – the text type will normally suffice unless it is an 'arty-crafty' publication. If the opening paragraph can be kept to a dozen or so words then interest is sharpened and the reader is on the writer's side from the start.

Aim for short sentences

Short sentences aid readability; anything up to thirty words is easy to follow and assimilate. There are obviously occasions when this can and should be exceeded, particularly for technical and scientific subjects; but even here, aim for brevity unless detailed explanation is required.

Keep your paragraphs short if you are writing for the popular and tabloid press. Five five-word lines is still the rule at the *Daily Mirror*, but for general publication work – leaflets, brochures and the like – the aim should be for perhaps three or four sentences in each paragraph. Even the occasional one-line sentence of a few words would not be out of place in a sales leaflet.

Guidelines on paragraphing

One of the main factors affecting readability is the length of paragraphs and where they are placed in the text. Short paragraphs (pars or paras to journalists) attract and hold the reader's attention, while excessively long ones tend to be unreadable and fail to communicate. Just look at a page of typescript that is unrelieved by paragraph breaks: it immediately seems to be indigestible and stuffy. Compare that with a page broken up by lively headings which straightaway appears more interesting and inviting.

Paragraphs allow the writer to change tack or subject and, equally important, give the eye a rest. When the text moves from one point to another that is the time for a par break. However, much will depend on the style of the publication or document and on the column width. For news-style print jobs, using double or multi-column format, paragraph breaks are usually needed after every second or third sentence – say about every 50 to 70 words. At make-up stage, this will allow subheadings to be inserted and columns to be equalized or space filled with displayed quotes. For single-column reports, books, manuals, leaflets and brochures, it is usually better to have longer paragraphs with perhaps four or five sentences. There should be at least two par breaks per column, otherwise you are back to that grey look again.

Short paragraphs are best for news releases; if each has a significant fact, then the release will stand a much better chance of being used than a long, stodgy one. The same applies to speeches which may be issued along with the release. An occasional single-sentence paragraph can have an electrifying effect on the text, especially if it is a technical or heavy-going subject. But, on the other hand, too many jerky, staccato paragraphs can distract and confuse the reader. As with everything else, it is a case of moderation.

Where to place the par break? This requires some skill: it is no use pressing the return key and hoping for the best. A paragraph is a unit of thought, not of length, says Fowler. But in news-style publications and certainly in news releases, it is the other way round: the paragraph is essentially a unit of length with maybe six or seven par breaks per page of copy, possibly more in some cases.

The best place for a break is where the text can be neatly divided without upsetting the word flow, say three or four per page of typescript, with one linked to the other in a seamless way. If a natural link is not there, then use an appropriate conjunction like *but, moreover, however*; otherwise recast the sentence at the break and refer back. But you will usually be able to find suitable points to break the text without editing. Try to have a mix of short and slightly longer sentences to produce a change of pace and give colour to the copy. Too many short ones can irritate the reader, but too many long ones can bore and tire the eye.

Some final points in relation to DTP typesetting: try to leave at least three words on the last line of a paragraph; try to avoid starting a new paragraph on the last line of a page. Indents for typescript and typesetting should not be more than three or four characters' width; if they go in too far the par break will be over-emphasized, although some designers may prefer to do this deliberately for special effect. Intros and first paragraphs after headings usually go full out (to the full column width) with subsequent par breaks indented. Don't leave a 'widow' with a few characters dangling at the top of a page: *-ed* or *-der* hanging overhead look awful. Try to fill the line out by adding words, or cutting and taking the overhang back.

Line width and type size

As for column width, try not to have more than 45 characters per line, including spaces and punctuation; anything above that tends to give a 'stringy' look. If the copy is set across the page, aim for between 70 and 80 characters per line. But remember that lines with only a few characters, those that run round a photograph or display heading for example, will be awkward to read and look messy.

Be careful when considering the relationship between line length and type size. Much will depend on your design objectives and the purpose of your printwork. As a general guide for ease of reading, type should not be much smaller than 10pt, or perhaps 9pt at a pinch if well line-spaced. A line of 45 characters of 10pt Times, for example, gives a very readable 70mm column width.

Headings provide interest

Solid lumps of type will put the reader off. If for some reason you cannot break up the text with par breaks and/or illustrations, insert subheadings (also called crossheadings). These are of inferior weight to the main heading or title and give the eye a break from line after line of characters. They also add interest to the piece by flagging up new points the writer wishes to bring out.

Subheadings should be either in a larger size and/or perhaps in bold so as to stand out from the rest of the text. Make sure there are not too many on a page. If they are scattered about willy-nilly they look untidy, and might even look as if they are just there to fill space (which they might well be!). When you insert headings, balance them so as to avoid 'rivering' with one adjacent to another. In news-style publications, one-word subheadings look best, preferably of not more than seven or eight characters.

The best time to insert subheadings is at first proof stage; if they go in too early you will not know where they will fall when the type has been set. Avoid having a subhead above the last line of a column: put it in higher up or cut it out. Headlines can also go in at proof stage. It is useful to have a working heading when the copy is written to help with identification later on.

Line and letter spacing

Space between lines is called 'leading' (pronounced *ledding*) from the time when a strip of metal – usually a casting in lead – was inserted between each line of hand-composed type, or automatically added to the line in machine typesetting. Leading is said to increase readability by 12 per cent as it introduces what the designer calls 'air' into the solid text, making it easier on the eye.

But avoid too much space between lines: that can be as bad as not enough, for the text will be harder, not easier, to read. And the wider the text is set, the more leading is needed for good readability. Where there is no leading at all, the text is said to be 'set solid'. The spacing is specified in point sizes (for example, 1pt or 2pt, with 72 points to the inch). Make sure that this line-by-line spacing is consistent; this is particularly important when setting text for reproduction by DTP.

Software packages enable the DTP operator to select line spacing leading in point sizes and to perform many other typographical settings like line justification and widths, variable type sizes and a wide selection of faces, as well as extended and condensed styles. Underlining is another option, but care is needed in order to avoid it 'colliding' with the line underneath.

Pay close attention to the spacing between characters, or what the printer would call letterspacing. This is another software option and some DTP machines and word processors will insert letterspacing automatically in order to fill out the line, particularly when copy is set justified with both edges aligned. Letterspacing can be adjusted for readability and aesthetics or to fill a certain area, and is most often used for lines of capitals for display. Special typographic effects can be obtained by removing or adding space between characters to produce what is known as 'kerning'.

Where to break

End-of-line word division often causes trouble, and words can get misread if they are broken at the wrong place. Once the prerogative of the compositor, word breaks are now mostly computer controlled but they can still go wrong: at worst a single character gets turned over; at best a typographical eyesore. When the copy is keyed in, the operator tells the computer to hyphenate and take over a set number of characters for a given line width. Some software options allow the operator to override automatic hyphenation and insert word breaks manually.

Computers sometimes get it right but more often do not. And then the word processor operator shuts off the automatic mode and goes to hyphensearch, relying on fading memories of how to break words at the right place. According to *Hart's Rules* which gives a number of examples, word breaks should be avoided. One way is to set copy ranged left and ragged right; this will mean fewer word breaks than if the type matter is justified with both margins aligned and with the ends of the lines ranged with one another.

Unless you have lines ending with longish words (ten or more characters) there is seldom any need for a break when using ragged right setting. At proof stage avoid hyphenated line endings by simply taking a word over to the next line. Avoid uneven word spacing, when the computer struggles to complete a line and thus breaks where it can.

Where word breaks are unavoidable, etymology and pro-nunciation are the main determinants. Divide words at obvious syllable breaks, as in *atmo-sphere* or *trans-port*, or where two consonants come together like *forget-ting, minis-ter* and *estab-lish*. If there is one consonant at the break point, that character is normally taken over as with *Euro-pean, popu-lar*.

Do not divide two consonants forming one sound (*calm-est, fea-ther*). The endings -*ism*, -*ist* and -*istic* are usually taken over and so are -*ing* present participles like *target-ing*. (But note *puz-zling, trick-ling*.) Do not carry over -*ted* or -*ded*. Be careful to reject divisions that could confuse or change the meaning: legends not leg-ends, re-adjust not read-just. A divided word should never end a page, especially a right hand one. A word should not be broken at the end of a paragraph to leave the last line with a hyphen and a few characters. Many more examples will be found in *Hart's Rules* and in the *Collins Gem Dictionary of Spelling and Word Division*.

Choice of typeface

Choosing the appropriate typeface is quite complex as much depends on the subject matter and style of the work. However, here are some ground rules worth considering: one is that serif types (those where the letter strokes are finished off like Times or Bodoni) are easier to read line after line than sans serif typefaces like Gill and Helvetica.

Set type so that it reads with the minimum of effort and eyestrain; each job presents different problems depending on the type style being used. The professional designer or typographer will gauge the most appropriate typeface for any given job by taking into account the target audience and subjects covered.

Printing considerations

Without going into the broad subject of design, it is important to remember that ideas that might look great on a visual sometimes fail to work when they get into print. For instance, it is next to useless reversing large amounts of text out of a solid colour (say white out of black) or out of a photograph as this guarantees non-readability. A few lines of display type set fairly large can be read without difficulty, but when it comes to lines of text set solid in 10pt or smaller, there will be an immediate switch-off.

Similarly, don't try to print a tinted typeface over a tinted page of equal strength. And don't try to print yellow type on

8 Point

DESIGN AS APPLIED TO PRINTED MATTER IS THE MEANING
ful arrangement of the elements in a page or other visual area. The
arrangement serves as an invisible scaffolding or framework on which
to display meanings in print and picture. The contribution of the

9 Point

DESIGN AS APPLIED TO PRINTED MATTER IS THE
meaningful arrangement of the elements in a page or other
visual area. The arrangement serves as an invisible scaffolding
or framework on which to display meanings in print and pic

10 Point

DESIGN AS APPLIED TO PRINTED MATTER IS THE
meaningful arrangement of the elements in a page or
other visual area. The arrangement serves as an invis
ible scaf folding or framework on which to display

11 Point

DESIGN AS APPLIED TO PRINTED MATTER IS
the meaningful arrangement of the elements in
a page or other visual area. The arrangement
serves as an invisible scaffolding or framework on

12 Point

DESIGN AS APPLIED TO PRINTED MATT
er is the meaningful arrangement of the
elements in a page or other visual area. The
arrangement serves as an invisible scaffolding

14 Point

DESIGN AS APPLIED TO PRINTED
matter is the meaningful arrangement
of the ele ments in a page or other

16 Point

DESIGN AS APPLIED TO PRINT
ed matter is the meaningful arr
angement of the elements in a pa

18 Point

DESIGN AS APPLIED TO PRI

Figure 6.1 *Comparison between a serif type (Baskerville) and
non-serif (Gill Sans) in medium and bold styles, 8pt to 32pt sizes*

20 Point

DESIGN AS APPLIED TO printed matter is the mean ingful arrangement of the

22 Point

DESIGN AS APPLIED T o printed matter is the meaningful arrangement

24 Point

DESIGN AS APPLIED to printed matter is the meaningful arrangeme

28 Point

DESIGN AS APPLI ed to printed matt er is the meaningfu

32 Point

DESIGN AS APP

Figure 6.1 *continued.*

8 Point
DESIGN AS APPLIED TO PRINTED MATTER IS THE MEANING
ful arrangement of the elements in a page or other visual area. The
arrangement serves as an invisible scaffolding or framework on
which to display meanings in print and picture. The contribution

9 Point
DESIGN AS APPLIED TO PRINTED MATTER IS THE
meaningful arrangement of the elements in a page or other
visual area. The arrangement serves as an invisible scaf
folding or framework on which to display meanings in print

10 Point
DESIGN AS APPLIED TO PRINTED MATTER IS
the meaningful arrangement of the elements in a page
or other visual area. The arrangement serves as an
invisible scaffolding or framework on which to display

11 Point
DESIGN AS APPLIED TO PRINTED MATTER
is the meaningful arrangement of the elements
in a page or other visual area. The arrangement
serves as an invisible scaffolding or framework on

12 Point
DESIGN AS APPLIED TO PRINTED MAT
ter is the meaningful arrangement of the
elements in a page or other visual area. The
arrangement serves as an invisible scaffolding

14 Point
DESIGN AS APPLIED TO PRINTED
matter is the meaningful arrangement
of the elements in a page or other vis

16 Point
DESIGN AS APPLIED TO PRIN
ted matter is the meaningful arr
angement of the elements in a

18 Point
DESIGN AS APPLIED TO P

Figure 6.1   *continued.*

65

20 Point

DESIGN AS APPLIED TO PRI nted matter is the meaningful arrangement of the element in

22 Point

DESIGN AS APPLIED TO P rinted matter is the meanin gful arrangement of the ele

24 Point

DESIGN AS APPLIED T o printed matter is the meaningful arrangement o

28 Point

DESIGN AS APPLIED to printed matter is the meaningful arrang

32 Point

DESIGN AS APPLI

Figure 6.1 *continued.*

white paper, or any pastel shades on white for that matter. Tinted papers often give readability problems and it is generally better to stick to black on white, using colour either as solids or as tints for headings and display panels.

Include illustrations if possible

If the job is text-intensive and in danger of looking 'stodgy' it is advisable to include illustrations – either line drawings, photographs or perhaps explanatory panels which can be overprinted in colour. All illustrations should of course be captioned unless they are simply for decoration. The reader will often ignore the text and only look at the photograph or drawing. Captions are read twice as much as the text and turn glancers and page-flippers into readers. Annual reports are a typical example of this.

Break up the monotony of long blocks of copy by using the ornaments and symbols provided by most software packages. If there are a series of facts it is better to number them rather than trying to interconnect them. Always try to think of ways to attract the reader's eye, in ways appropriate to the content.

Justified or ragged right?

Both styles have their advantages, and all designers have their own ideas on whether the one is more readable than the other. It depends largely on the style of publication: if it is a 'newsy' one then the justified style would probably be better for that is the way most newspapers set their type. On the other hand, brochures and leaflets usually look more attractive and are easier for the reader to follow when set ragged right. But there are no firm rules and it is up to the designer to produce an acceptable style directed at the target audience and within the house style pattern of the publishing organization.

Bold and italics

Bold type helps the reader to identify subject changes and gives the printed page visual interest. It provides focal points among roman and non-bold typefaces. But again it is a case of everything in moderation: too much bold type destroys the impact of a few carefully positioned subheadings. As a general rule do not use bold type in any great quantity, except perhaps for a display panel. Nearly all typefaces will have fonts in boldface, and most computers and word processors will have the facility to change from 'plain' type to bold or italics, and to some other type styles as well.

Individual words in a run of text should not be set in bold just for stress, for that is the job of italics. But if too many words are italicized, or even whole sentences or complete paragraphs, this method of providing emphasis ceases to work. Fowler is scornful of overuse: 'Printing a passage in italics, like under-lining one in a letter, is a primitive way of soliciting attention' says the second edition.

The main uses of italics are listed in *Hart's Rules*. These include titles of books, names of ships, newspapers and magazines, titles of TV and radio programmes, films and foreign words and phrases not fully naturalized in English. However, modern style trends suggest that the italics style within text is being used less frequently, particularly for foreign words and for titles of periodicals.

Using the designer to the best advantage

Choice of designer is crucial: get the wrong one and you have wasted valuable time and probably spent money you could ill afford. Take two views on this important subject – one from a communications consultant and the other from an organization with its own studio. The first comes from consultant and editor Peter C Jackson:

Any editor worth their salt should have a basic knowledge of the most effective way to present their words to the reader. But sooner or later they must commit their precious sentences to the expert hand of the graphic designer.

It is always worth taking time and trouble to seek out a designer who will be sympathetic to your overall objectives. There are those who have a purely visual approach to publication design; they see your deathless prose as merely slabs of grey matter to balance illustrations and white space. Use them at your peril.

Seek out (by example or recommendation) those designers with a flair for words themselves. They will be able to meld words, pictures and display type into an imaginative and satisfying whole. There is no finer working partnership than a writer and a designer who each appreciate and respect the other's experience and skills. That is a combination worth pursuing.

Next, the view from Pira International, the Surrey-based research and technology centre for the printing, packaging, paper and publishing industries. Jason Dronfield, Pira's designer, says that regardless of the type of job, before a single word is read, the layout, colours and typography must form an immediate impression that will entice and excite the eye. 'And it is that first impression that counts more than anything else'.

It is crucial that the designer is properly briefed on the objective, tone of the message and target audience of the publication, brochure or leaflet – no matter what it is. If the typography and layout reflect and support the message conveyed then the text stands a much better chance of being read. Dronfield feels that a 'busy' layout, possibly with a combination of complementary typefaces, would be suitable for a leaflet describing a new product; whereas a brochure describing an expensive management training course would project a more 'upmarket' image by using a sans serif typeface printed on high quality paper with plenty of white space.

'A page of text without headings is uninviting and disorientating to the reader,' he says. 'Signpost headings in a different typeface or bullet points are effective in directing the reader to changes of thought or subject.'

Readability is probably the most important factor in the design of any publication no matter how it is printed. Paying attention to it is the communicator's first priority.

7

Headlines: making them work

Headlines are a crucial element in printed communication. Short, punchy headings attract attention and take the eye to the text. However well the words have been crafted, they will not be read if the reader isn't encouraged to move on. That is the job of the headline: style will depend on the audience and type of publication. Newspaper format house journals and periodicals demand a brisk, urgent approach. Leaflets and brochures require a different kind of headline, as do internal and contact reports.

Whatever the type of publication or report, the headline must encapsulate the main points of the text in an interesting and eye-catching way. In fact, the livelier the better. Space will always be a limiting factor, and this is why it is often difficult to achieve a newsy yet informative headline within the constraints of the column or page widths. That, of course, is where skill and experience come in.

House journals must be in tune with the audience to which the publication is addressed. A study of the many journal styles to be seen today will help you when you edit and produce

newsfile
WINTER 1996/97

IPA

waving not drowning!

First indications are that agency employment figures continue to rise

The 1996 IPA Agency Census shows another increase in agency employment figures. This is borne out by IPA Stage 1 - for trainees - which saw all records broken. There were 180 delegates for the autumn course versus 120 in 1994 and 62 in 1992. The full census report, which includes breakdowns by job and gender, is due out mid January.

On the down side, the summary from the confidential 1996 IPA Agency Costs Analysis shows a continuing squeeze on margins to December 1995 and to March 1996 with gross income at 11.78% of billing (versus 12.14% the previous year) and net profit from advertising activities at 1.60% of billing (versus 1.64%).

Said IPA Director General Nick Phillips: "There is a very positive atmosphere in the agencies at the moment. Despite the real concerns about margin pressures, turnover growth is allowing investment in new people and new systems and an enthusiasm for new media solutions. The IPA is continuing to invest in increased training and effectiveness initiatives to ensure that the agency contribution to clients' business success is properly recognised."

Said Peter Walker, Financial Director of Ogilvy & Mather and Chairman of the IPA Finance Policy Group:

"The fall in margins indicates how the industry is being squeezed at either end – squeezed from consultants at the top end and cheap production houses at the bottom end. There are a number of ways we can protect our margins. And we must protect our margins. I think the investment in training at the junior level is a positive move forward to re-establish ourselves at the core of the marketing community." ■

page one

Figure 7.1 *Use of lower case type for this headline shows the designer has a modern approach to style*

publications whether current or new. Newspaper and magazine headings reveal many contrasting forms, with the tabloids shouting the news and the 'heavies' taking a more staid and thoughtful line. The trade press, professional and scientific journals each adopt differing styles to reflect the varying needs and interests of their audiences.

There are no set rules for writing headlines, as every publication requires different treatment. The following basic guidelines for creating and presenting headlines will provide the foundation for a usable and flexible style which can be adapted according to individual needs.

Present tense for news-style publications

The headline is essential for effective communication and to arrest the reader's attention. Its job is to take the eye to the story, to whet the appetite, to excite and inform. In-house newspapers or newsletters headlines should contain a present-tense verb, and thus generally follow newspaper style. Participle *-ing* endings should be avoided as in 'XYZ company is *launching* a new product.' It is much better to write 'XYZ company *launches...*' While the former is passive, slow and boring, the latter is vibrant and active. Most people read newspapers, and so it makes sense to follow their style whenever possible.

Headlines work best when they have an active, 'doing' verb, preferably single syllable ones like *calls, tells, says, goes*. The heading should say what the story is about in a few short words, enough to make the reader to want to find out more, and there are plenty of examples of two- or three-word headlines that work well.

But there are occasions when just one word can have a dramatic effect and take the reader to the heart of the story like GOTCHA! (during the Falklands war) and GRABALOT (pay rises and bonuses for Camelot directors). Headlines like these, which appear regularly in the tabloid press take much thought, but are extremely effective in telling a story in a punchy, pithy way.

It is important that headlines should stand on their own and not become part of the following copy, for example a house journal headline might read 'John Smith, new managing director of XYZ company,' with the first line of the copy running on directly from it saying 'Has plans for expansion...' Headlines should never do that.

Questions and humour

Another way to spark interest is to write question headings from time to time, starting with *Who, Why, Where, What,* or constructions like *Is it, Was it.* For publications containing mostly feature material, take a softer line. You can use longer headings and perhaps even leave out the verb. Jokey headlines, like HELLO TO GOOD BUYS in women's pages, work best in tabloid-style newspapers and house journals, but can dilute the meaning of a serious message. If used sparingly, headings like PURRFECT ENDING for a story about cats about to use up their nine lives, and MONEY TO BYRNE for a news item announcing a two-million pound pools winner can get a story over far more effectively than a straightforward heading. Look for headings with a play on words, the *double entendre.* But avoid being facetious, and while there can be no objection to the occasional pun, attempts at being funny can cause a groan and be seen as a poor form of wit. It is all a question of balance, and fitting headlines to the audience and message. There is always room for humour.

Avoid 'label' headings

'Label' headings make a bland statement without verb or verve and hold little interest for the reader. They produce an effect of dullness and monotony. A heading which announces the winners of an awards scheme SMITH WINS TOP AWARD is so much better than the bland statement AWARDS ANNOUNCED – a typical label heading.

Do not use label headings above feature articles in house magazines or in newsletters. They can, however, be used as signposts for sectioning off a publication: labels like *Latest publications* or *Future events* are quite acceptable for this purpose.

Headings in sales leaflets and brochures

Sales leaflets, company brochures, catalogues and manuals require hard sell and persuasive messages. You can borrow a lot from the language of advertising. David Ogilvy, founder of the Ogilvy and Mather agency, writing in *Confessions of an Advertising Man*, says that five times as many people read the headline as the text. He goes on:'The wickedest of all sins is to run an advertisement *without* a headline.' And then he adds something that could cause the writer of a sales leaflet to take a deep inward breath: 'If you haven't done some selling in your headline, you have wasted 80 per cent of your client's money.'

The two most powerful words in a headline are *free* and *new*. Other words and phrases useful for headlines are: *advance, advice/help on, bargain, big/great/huge, development, easy, fast/ quick, gain, hurry, important, just out, profit/loss, quality, says/ tells, win, want/need*. Avoid superlatives like *amazing, magic, miraculous, revolutionary, sensational, superb, startling* unless they are for an advertisement.

Emotion can play a significant part in a successful and memorable headline: Ogilvy suggests that headlines can be strengthened by words like *darling, love, fear, proud, friend, baby*. He quotes a headline of a few decades ago for a range of soaps and moisturizers with a girl talking to her lover on the telephone: DARLING, I'M HAVING THE MOST EXTRA-ORDINARY EXPERIENCE... I'M HEAD OVER HEELS IN DOVE as being one of the most provocative headlines ever to come out of O&M. More recent examples of memorable headlines include CATISFACTION (Whiskas petfoods) and CHANNEL FUNNEL (P&O European Ferries).

For sales leaflets and other promotional material, a good headline is one which makes a stated promise and a well-defined benefit, is not set at an angle so that the reader gets neck-ache trying to read it, and is set in easy-to-read type. Headlines using an unfamiliar typeface and those that are buried in the text and printed upside down just to satisfy a creative whim should be ruled out immediately.

Style and presentation

While short, snappy headings are suitable for news-style publications, longer ones are sometimes more appropriate for sales leaflets and brochures. According to Ogilvy, when the New York University School of Retailing ran headline tests for a big department store, they found that headlines of ten words or more, and containing news and information, consistently sold more merchandise than short ones.

Presentation is important. Bold type, at least seven or eight sizes larger than the text type (or up as subs would say) makes the headline stand out from the rest of the text. For instance, if the copy was set in 10pt, 2pt leaded, headings of 18pt or larger would provide sufficient contrast. Although it is a matter of individual style and taste, most headlines look better if set upper and lower case rather than full capitals. A long headline of four or more words in capitals adds nothing to the effectiveness of the message. Do not underline or put capitals in an attempt to add emphasis: this will not have the desired effect and will look old-fashioned and clumsy.

Don't put a full stop at the end of a headline. Make sure that if a headline runs to more than one line that the first is not broken with a hyphen: that looks not only ghastly but thoroughly unprofessional. Either shorten the line so that there is no need to break the last word or rewrite the whole heading. Try not to exceed three-line headings for newspaper-style publications (three-deck in journalese) although a four-deck heading in a large size, say 42pt or more, would not look out of place in a tabloid format.

Nowadays, DTP allows great flexibility in choice of headline styles and sizes, and there is no limit to the creative possibilities that can be achieved. The time taken on the writing and presentation of headlines is well worthwhile and deserves as much care and attention as the story itself. Subheadings, or crossheads, are just as important as their bigger brothers and demand just as much care in their wording and presentation.

28 Point

DESIGN AS APPLI
ed to printed matter
is the meaningful ar

32 Point

DESIGN AS APP
lied to printed
matter is the mea

36 Point

DESIGN AS A
pplied to print
ed matter is the

Figure 7.2 *Helvetica medium in sizes suitable for headlines*

DESIGN AS APPLIED TO PRINTED MATTER IS THE
meaningful arrangement of the elements in a page or
other visual area. The arrangement serves as an invis
ible scaffolding or framework on which to display mean

DESIGN AS APPLIED
to printed matter is the
meaningful arrangeme

**DESIGN AS APPLIED TO PRINTED MATTER IS
the meaningful arrangement of the elements in
a page or other visual area. The arrangement
serves as an invis ible scaffolding or framework**

DESIGN AS APPLIE
d to printed matter is
the meaningful arra

Figure 7.3 *Contrasts in type sizes and styles in Helvetica
medium and bold*

Subheadings

Subheadings (also called crossheadings) can be centred or
ranged left and are a good way to break up long stretches of
type. Pages look better with subheads and they can be handy for
filling space, for instance when you have difficulty in equalizing
column depths. Too many subheads will look messy, particularly if the page is no larger than A4.

Subheads should consist of one or two words of not more than seven or eight characters each; they should never go into a second line. Do not have them in the same type style as the text. They work best if they are in bold type or in italics. Sometimes they look well in a second colour: it will not add to the cost if printed in one of the colours already being used. Like headlines, subheads do not require full stops at the end, but there is no objection to question or exclamation marks.

Extra emphasis can be given to a passage by inserting side-headings in the margins. Insert these at layout stage and do not attempt to write them in when the body copy for the text is written. Style and layout design will dictate how many there should be and where they should be positioned.

Never overlook the wording and presentation of headings. Time and trouble spent getting them right will always pay off: improved communication will inevitably result.

8

Dealing with figures and abbreviations

Figuring out the numbers

Style for numbers is as important as for words. A mixture of numeral styles can confuse the reader and make the production look amateurish. A set style for numbers should be a priority for everything produced whether for print, presentation, release or correspondence.

Style books set out a number of guidelines. These mostly follow *Hart's Rules* which gives plenty of examples. Individual publications adapt and expand on these to suit their own needs and audiences. While rules of this nature are open to interpretation, they provide a starting point and this section draws attention to some of the important points for house style.

Basic considerations

The first rule is not to start a sentence with a figure. Spell it out instead. The reason for this is that the style is followed almost universally in newspapers and magazines and in most professionally produced publications. It is something we have all become used to and any diversion immediately stands out and looks 'wrong'. But it would be clumsy to spell out a multi-digit number; either write out *The year 1997* or else recast the sentence completely. However, there are occasions when it is difficult to avoid a figure at the beginning and when this happens, say in an annual report or in giving statistical data, then there may be no alternative but to start with a figure.

The second rule – and this is for numbers *within* a sentence – is to spell out numbers up to and including ten; above that write figures. But if there are sequences of numbers, some of which may be higher than ten, use figures throughout for the sake of consistency and clarity. Write out *hundredth* but after that put *101st* and so on. For decimals, use a full stop on the line as in *1.5*, and do not attempt to centralize it as if writing a decimal by hand. (In other languages a decimal comma is used.) There is no point in putting a single zero after the decimal point unless it is called for in tabular matter, but a nought should go before the point as in *0.75*. Numerals should be used for page references, currencies and for groups of statistics.

Symbols, abbreviations and punctuation

Next: avoid using the % sign in text, spell out *per cent* as two words, but use *percentage* of course. The symbol should be kept for tables and charts and for text where figures predominate. Fractions should be hyphenated (*two-thirds*) and do not mix (or compare) fractions with decimals. When both a whole number and a fraction are spelt out, only hyphenate the fraction as in *one and three-quarters*. It is better to write (in formal text) *twentieth century* rather than *20th*, note that *one in three* is singular but *two in five* are plural. Some newspapers will prefer to write *a mile and a half* instead of *one and a half miles*, but seldom, if ever, print *1½* miles!

Avoid a combination of the *to/from* style (when comparing years, for instance) with hyphens as in *from 1997–98*; put *from two to three*, or *from 12 to 13*, but not a mixture of the two styles.

Reserve hyphens or dashes for numerals and never use them for spelt-out figures.

A *billion* at one time meant a million million but modern usage suggests that it means a *thousand million* – a definition accepted by most, if not all, national newspapers. It is better to spell out a million and a billion, but if *m* and *bn* are used do not put a full point after the abbreviations unless they come at the end of a sentence. Full points should not follow units of weight and measurement (*cm, ft, kg*), and do not put hyphens in combinations like *half an inch* or *half a dozen*. With temperature put the degree symbol immediately before *C* or *F*. No punctuation is necessary in dates (*12 March 1997*). In compounds, put a hyphen in *half-hour* and *two-day*.

Nouns of measurement and quantity: singular or plural?

All nouns of measurement remain singular when used attributively: *a six-foot man, a five-litre can.* But plural feet or inches are used where an adjective follows, as in *he is six feet tall, she is five feet six inches.* Similarly, *stone* stays singular in plural expressions, as in *she weighs nine stone.* Unless used attributively metric measurements always take the plural form as in *the tank has a capacity of ten litres.*

Nouns of quantity – *score, dozen, hundred* – take the singular form if qualified by a preceding word: *two thousand will be sufficient.* But they will be plural when denoting indefinite amounts as in *the company publishes hundreds of publications.* Measurements of quantity and distance containing a plural noun can be taken as being singular and therefore take a singular verb: *twenty pounds/miles is too expensive/far.*

It is worth noting that the word 'number' takes a plural verb when it refers to a quantity or group as in *a number of people were...* but when it means a figure it takes the singular: *two hundred pounds is the number I quoted.* So much for figures.

Abbreviations: the long and the short of it

Now let's look at abbreviations and how to deal with them. First, the abbreviation everyone uses without hesitation: *OK*. What do the letters stand for? Unless you have read it in the 'Verbals' column of the *IPR Journal* or made a study of the subject, the chances are that you don't know – and that is the trouble with using abbreviations: readers may not know what a given set of initials stand for and that means communication not working.

OK, here are some answers. Take your pick: originating from the nineteenth century, it could come from Old Kinderhook, the upstate New York birthplace of eighth American president Van Buren who used the initials as an election slogan; or perhaps a contraction of American slang *Orl Korrect*, or of Orrins-Kendall crackers, according to Bill Bryson in *Mother Tongue*. Even though the origin may be obscure, we all know what the letters mean.

Few abbreviations are as familiar and instantly understandable as OK. Abbreviations are often used without hesitation, but are meaningless to the reader, simply because the writer is used to them and they have become part of the company's jargon. Get them wrong and your message fails. So what are the rules for dealing with them?

Avoid overuse

The first point, to quote a well-known saying, is familiarity breeds contempt. If you overuse abbreviated sets of initials they quickly tire the eye. Unless the initials are sufficiently familiar to be part of the language (BBC, CBI, TUC) the name should be spelt out in full before using abbreviations. It would be equally tiring to see a repetition of the full name when a contraction would be more suitable and convenient. On the other hand, there would be little point in explaining the initials BMW, because besides being a well-known brand, there is usually no *need* for the reader to know what they mean.

Do not continue to use the same set of initials. For example, in references to the BBC use 'the Corporation' or possibly for informal speech or tabloid publication, 'the Beeb'. Again, for the CBI, it could be called after the first reference 'the employers' organization' or just 'the organization'. In other cases, use a shortened form such as institute/association/ federation/body or, in the case of firms, company/consultancy/ firm/group/shop/store, or name by product or service type. But keep clear of slang words like *outfit/shop* for public relations or advertising firms.

Be careful of ambiguities

Watch out for ambiguities like PC which could mean personal computer, Police Constable or Privy Counsellor. You may be *in* PR, but you are not *a* PR. You see an *ad* but not an *advert*, you join a *demo* and you get *flu* not *the* (and no apostrophe). Ensure that descriptions are accurate. A common mistake is for BSI to be written out as the British Standards *Institute* instead of *Institution*. Writers wonder how to write PLC (Public Limited Company). It is up to the company: it can be shown in caps, or lower case or a mixture of the two, although it seems that the all-capitals style, either in roman or italics, is the one generally favoured.

Capitals and full stops

Most house styles require all abbreviations to be set in capitals, but some organizations are read as acronyms and take lower case (*Aslef* for instance), while others are set upper and lower case for the sake of clarity (*BSc, Dr*). In general, full stops are not needed in abbreviations of company names, titles and civil honours, academic qualifications, and the courtesy titles of *Mr/ Mrs/Ms*.

No full point follows numerical abbreviations (*1st/2nd*), units of length, weight or time (*cm/ft/cwt/lb/kg/min/sec*); *am/pm*; days of the week (*Mon/Tues*); months (*Aug/Dec*); or in points of the compass (*NE/SW*) unless used separately (*N.S.E.W.*). They are seldom necessary in acronyms (*laser*) and if there is no way of avoiding *etc* (never *&c*) don't put a point after it.

Make sure your text or office-produced documents have all abbreviations typed or set in a consistent way without (or with) full points as may be dictated by house style. Get out of the habit of using *eg, ie, pa* – they are what might be termed 'lazyisms'. For *etc* write a short listing of what the items are; for *eg/ie* just put a comma, for *pa* spell out *per annum* or *annually* or *every/each year*.

Ampersands and definite articles

The ampersand is a useful and convenient abbreviation for *and*, but it should be restricted to company names (*Marks & Spencer*) and never used as an alternative to *and* in text. A check with the telephone directory will confirm whether or not a company name contains an ampersand.

If a shortened word is pronounced, do not put a definite article before it (*the* IPR but not *the M&S*). Hence the rule: *the* goes with abbreviated organizations but not with company names. You wouldn't write *the ICI* would you? Be careful in exchanging *phone* for telephone, *photo* for photograph as both contractions are more comfortable when used informally and in speech.

A full guide to abbreviations (but only covering the larger commercial organizations) will be found in *The Oxford Writers' Dictionary*; advice on setting abbreviations for printed material is given in *Hart's Rules*. Most dictionaries will indicate what abbreviated titles, honours and qualifications stand for. And, by the way, *OWD* prefers OK to *okay*.

9

Keep it short, simple – and plain

Some of the strictures of purists who insist upon rigid adherence to rules of grammar are little more than mythology and have no place in everyday usage. Those who believe that it is always wrong to split an infinitive, end a sentence with a preposition, or start with a conjunction are in a linguistic straitjacket and unable to communicate as well as they might. Likewise, unnecessarily long words, complex sentences and lengthy paragraphs confuse the reader. Double negatives, needless jargon, faulty or misplaced punctuation, and constant repetition of words and ideas can all lead to nonsensical, hard-to-follow text. And that means that the reader quickly loses interest in the face of endless waffle.

Plain English, written in a simple and straightforward way, is the recipe for clarity of expression. More than that, it is the basis of good style. Earlier chapters have discussed some of the ingredients for securing and keeping the reader reading, and, without trespassing on that territory this chapter looks at writing with economy of language, a crucial factor in getting your message understood.

Aim for brevity

Brevity is the essence, particularly for the media. Complicated constructions and lengthy, unwieldy sentences not only bore the reader, they provide an instant barrier to effective communication. More important still, brevity spells time saved for the reader. Copy must be clear, concise and unambiguous. Whether the piece is for publication in a newspaper or periodical or for a brochure or leaflet, it should be written so that it grips the reader from start to finish. What are the best ways of achieving this?

First, use short words rather than long, and plain language instead of complex terminology. Try to keep sentences down to 25 to 30 words, fewer if you can. Use full stops liberally: they are the writer's best friend. Aim for not more than three sentences per paragraph for releases and news-style publications. But variety is the spice: an occasional longer paragraph gives colour and balance to a piece. And the one-liner can be effective – it jerks the reader to attention.

Sentences can of course be much longer than this; indeed, those of up to 60 or so words are acceptable for technical or legal contexts where detailed explanation is required. If a sentence is starting to 'look' too long, and tops the 60 mark, break it up with stops, or insert quotations if appropriate. With feature articles and corporate brochures you can be more generous with words. But even then, be aware that the longer the sentence the more likely the reader will tire and skip the copy you have tried so hard to get right in terms of style and fact.

As you write, get into the habit of asking yourself 'Is there a shorter word that means the same thing? Is there a better word? Are any words sheer verbiage and should be cut out? Is every word doing a job and telling you something?' In short, write tight to write well.

Plain words

Your search for plain words and the removal of unnecessary ones will be aided by using *The Plain English Guide* by Martin Cutts. There are, he says, three main techniques for dealing with 'dross' to allow your information to 'shine more clearly': strike out useless words and leave only those that tell you something; prune the dead wood, grafting on the vigorous; rewrite completely. Cutts gives many examples of the overlong word or phrase, the useless word, and the officialese that defies understanding; as well as advice on how to rewrite lengthy and tedious text. When making cuts it is essential not to alter the sense in any way and to follow the basic rules of grammar.

With a little thought it is easy: see how ten words in the following sentence can be lost without altering the meaning:

XYZ company *had as its main objective the need* (wanted) to increase output by at least 10 per cent *in* this *current financial year*

Here, the words in italics can be deleted without changing the meaning. The single word 'wanted' takes the place of seven needless ones. Verbiage like this throughout a piece of several hundred words would turn off the reader after only a few paragraphs. Expressions that can easily be shortened include: *the question as to whether,* (use *whether*); *there is no doubt that* (put *no doubt* or *doubtless*); *in spite of the fact that* (replace with *though*); *owing to the fact that* (write *since* or *because*).

Cutts includes helpful lists of plain and short words and phrases. For example, he advises *facts/details* not particulars; *help* not facilitate; *idea* not concept; *buy* not purchase; *start/ begin,* not commence. Do not let long-winded phrases get the better of you: for instance, write *although* or *despite* instead of 'despite the fact that'. Sir Ernest Gowers in *The Complete Plain Words* demonstrates that simple prepositions can often replace wordy phrases: *if* for 'in case of' and *to* for 'with a view to'.

Look for active verbs; avoid contractions

The verb drives the text forward. First, look for single syllable verbs: *go*, not proceed; *about* not cooncerning; *show* not demonstrate. You *pitch* rather than compete, *know* rather than comprehend, *let* not permit. To *think* is better than to believe, to *ask* is better than to enquire. And so on. Choose active-voice verbs by putting the 'doer' – the person or thing doing the action – in front of the verb. It is much better to write 'XYZ consultancy wants new clients' instead of 'new clients are wanted by XYZ consultancy'.

Try to avoid using too many adverbs as qualifiers 'They are an indulgence, often a sign that noun and verb are not working properly,' says *The Times Guide to English Style and Usage*. Much the same can be said for adjectives; avoid those that are flowery and expansive: *rather, very, little* (unless referring to size), *pretty* for example – especially in news stories. Never use them in releases, unless they are part of a quote, and even then it is better to cut them out if you can.

When you need to save words and shorten copy, do not fall into the trap of using contractions of modal or auxiliary verbs like will/shall/would; and so write *you'll/you'd*, or *you're/you've*, *I'm*. This is fine for speech and informal writing but not for formal contexts; it looks sloppy and chatty. (On the other hand, *n't* is an acceptable contraction of *not* for all but very formal usage.)

Avoid foreign words or phrases – and Latin

Another barrier to understanding is using foreign words or phrases when an English one will do just as well. While it is true that many verbal imports are often just the words or phrases you want because there is no exact English equivalent, do not write above the head of the reader, who might think you are showing off.

Don't go Latin unless you have to: put *among others* not *inter alia*; *yearly* or *annually* not 'per annum'; *about*, not *circa*; *regarding*, not *vis-à-vis*. As a general rule, avoid Latin and be safe! And be on your guard against pomposity: write *before* not 'prior to'; *ultimately* not 'at the end of the day'; *but* or *however* rather than 'having said that'.

Double negatives

Guard against double or multiple negatives with too many un-words like *unnecessary* or *unless*; or putting more than one *avoid* or *cease* or phrases such as *less than* and *not more than* in one sentence. If you do, the meaning can become obscure and the reader has to struggle with negatives (or too many positives for that matter) in order to understand what you mean.

Beware 'myths'

According to Cutts in *The Plain English Guide*, some of the so-called 'rules' of grammar religiously followed by purists and scholars are little more than myths. It is these myths that are a further barrier to clarity of communication. They are the territory of the pedant and do not have a place in everyday writing and speech. The top-of-the-list myth says you should never split an infinitive. While most commentators agree that it is better to avoid a split, by putting an adverb or another word between *to* and the infinitive verb as in *to boldly go*, 'no absolute taboo' should be placed on it (*Fowler's Modern English Usage*). Cutts himself says: 'If you can't bring yourself to split an infinitive, at least allow others to do so.' There is nothing to stop you splitting an infinitive but be aware that it will irritate some people.

Another myth is the long-held theory that sentences must never end with a preposition. Cutts says a few 'fossils' still believe this, but agrees that some sentences do need to be recast, not because they break any rule but because they 'sound ugly'. It all depends on the degree of formality the writer wants to achieve: it would be pedantic to write or say '*To* whom am I talking?' when 'Who am I talking *to*?' would be more natural. If the preposition looks stranded and unrelated to the word to which it belongs (or *belongs to!*) then rewrite the sentence and put it where it sounds natural. The more formal the piece, the earlier the preposition goes in the sentence. But do not move it back just because you think you should follow the schoolroom rule.

A third myth is that sentences must never begin with *and* or *but*. Authors throughout history have ignored this so-called ban: Cutts notes that Jane Austen begins almost every page with *but*, and *OED* gives several examples of sentences in English literature beginning with *and*. In fact, sentences starting this way tend to have a sparkle absent in others, and are an effective way of adding emphasis to a point already made.

Tips for writing tight

Writing tight in a plain, easy-to-read style is hard work and demands ruthless pruning. Try to keep cross-references to a minimum; divide complicated copy into vertical lists rather than having a succession of semi-colons or commas; don't bury key words or phases in slabs of text unrelieved by headings; don't confuse the lay-reader with jargon or technical terms and don't use slang words in any formal sense.

Cut unnecessary words and choose vigorous verbs. *To be* and *to have* are often the only ones you need to achieve crispness. Make the punctuation work for you by dividing the copy into short manageable sections with liberal use of full stops. Create interest by asking questions – a technique more commonly found in articles and feature material than in news items – and include quotations if appropriate. Keep your sentences short, and have plenty of paragraph breaks. In a report or internal document organize points under headings.

Be careful not to duplicate words and phrases in the same paragraph. Repeating technical words may be unavoidable, but nothing is more off-putting than reading the same word over and over again. Look for alternatives in *Roget's Thesaurus* or the *Penguin Dictionary of Synonyms*. Sometimes you can find the word you want in a good dictionary.

There is still much to do. . .

Don't think that once you've finished the piece that is the end of it. The work should not get anywhere near your OUT tray until you have edited and polished it over and over again and convinced yourself there is no way it can be improved. The whole piece might need rewriting.

Sometimes you will be rushed and get no chance to recast a piece. But don't despair – if you are quick you will undoubtedly have time for a bit of editing. Unless you are working on a news-release or are up against a tight deadline, there is usually time for another draft. And don't think, 'Oh well there is still time to look at it again at proof stage.' That is fatal and can lead to mistakes, particularly for rush jobs.

Resist the temptation to say 'That will do.' Instead, see whether there is room for improvement. The answer must be 'yes' because everything you write can be bettered. It is up to you to put the effort into making it the best copy you have ever written, even if this means extensive surgery to the text. Today's word processors and computers make major changes like transferring paragraphs and rewriting long passages an easy task. Writing takes time and effort. But it's worth it.

10

Writing for the press

There are special requirements for preparing written material for publication in newspapers, consumer magazines and trade journals, and also for broadcast in news outlets. The news release is still the basic form of communication between an organization and its audience, and there are various rules and conventions that should be followed to ensure the material gets published and does not end up in the bin. In this chapter I uncover important points concerning the writing and issuing of news releases, and then turn to commissioned articles.

News releases: basic requirements

When you send out a release you want it to be published. Remember that national and regional newspapers, consumer magazines and trade journals, all receive hundreds or perhaps thousands of news stories every day all vying with press releases for every inch of space. Broadcasting media – BBC and ITV programmes and the many national and local radio stations – also have huge demands on their airtime for news items and, like the press, need information presented in a succinct way.

Your news will be in competition with information from many other sources, not least stories coming in from staff journalists, freelancers and news agencies. The essential points are that releases must be worthy of publication and able to attract the journalist's attention. Here are the main points to watch.

Headings

The release should be clearly identifiable as a communication for publication or broadcast, and should carry a heading such as 'News Release', 'Press Release', 'Press Notice', 'Press Information', 'Information from XYZ' or just 'News from XYZ'. If sent out by a consultancy, it must be made clear that it is issued on behalf of the client company or organization. Such headings should be in capitals or upper and lower case of not less than 18pt so as to stand out from the mass of other material on sub-editors' desks. Print the heading in the corporate colour, typeface and style of the issuing organization.

Essential information

Put the full name and address of the issuing organization, with telephone, fax numbers and e-mail/web site address (if there is one) in a prominent position. Type the date of issue. Give a contact name for further information, together with his/her telephone/fax numbers if different from the main switchboard numbers. Give also the contact's e-mail address. Always include an out-of-hours telephone number since many journalists are still working when you have left the office. It is not necessarily good PR for the managing director or chairman to get your calls when you should be talking to the media in the first place!

Titles

The title of the release should be typed (or word-processed) in bold capitals but not underlined. (Don't write a too-clever-by-half or facetious heading – it won't work!) It should say in as few words as possible what the release is about, and should not, if possible, run to more than one line. Use a present tense verb. If secondary subheadings or side-heads are needed, then these should be in upper and lower case, either in plain or bold type.

Some ideal examples of release titles are: GO-AHEAD FOR ROYAL OPERA HOUSE'S THEATRE PROPOSALS AT TOWER BRIDGE (Department of the Environment); GOVERNMENT ANNOUNCES NEW USER-FRIENDLY CROWN COPYRIGHT LICENCE FOR ELECTRONIC PUBLISHING SECTOR (Cabinet Office); BLUNKETT CUTS RED TAPE (Department for Education and Employment); THAMESLINK 2000 GOES PUBLIC (Railtrack); WALKERS CRISPS KICKS OFF SCOTTISH SPORTING HEROES PROMOTION (Walkers Snack Foods); NEW ECONOMIC SURVEY SHOWS IMPROVING PICTURE FOR PRINTING INDUSTRY (British Printing Industries Federation);ROTAPRINT INTRODUCE BUDGET SRA3 PRESS FOR UNDER £12,000 (Rotaprint International).

Content

Be brief and factual and keep sentences short. Two sentences per paragraph is about right, and often just one sentence will be enough to get a point over. The opening paragraph should contain the essence of the story and display the news. Here you must answer who?/ when?/ where? questions in the same way that a reporter is required to do. For example, if a company chairman has made a statement, give his name and position, the date (if you say 'today' put the date in brackets afterwards so there can be no mistake), where the statement was made, and if at a hotel, name it. A trick here is to put the last two details in a second paragraph saying Mr So and So was speaking on (date) and (where) to save cluttering up the opening paragraph with detail that might easily obscure the point of the story. Never write 'recently' but always give the date.

Following paragraphs should expand on the story. Try not to let the copy run over to a second page. It will make the sub-editor's job much easier if you start with the main point, fill in

NEWS RELEASE

The Advertising Association

Abford House, 15 Wilton Road, London SW1V 1NJ
Telephone: 0171-828 2771   Fax: 0171-931 0376
E-mail: Advert@dial.pipex.com

Embargo: Immediate   16th July 1997

ADVERTISING ASSOCIATION WELCOMES

ADOPTION OF LARIVE REPORT

The Advertising Association welcomes the adoption yesterday by the

European Parliament of the Larive Report on the European

Commission's Green Paper on Commercial Communications.

Lionel Stanbrook, Deputy Director-General, said:

"The result is very good from the UK advertising industry's point of view.

This endorsement by the European Parliament has given the Green

Paper a welcome new impetus in the right direction. We are delighted

that MEPs have rejected the new anti-industry hard line that European

consumer groups have recently adopted."

MEPs voted overwhelmingly to endorse Rapporteur Larive's position that

the 'country of origin' principle for commercial communications should be

maintained, and endorsed the majority of the European Commission's

proposals as set out in the Green Paper.

For further information please contact: **Lionel Stanbrook**, The

Advertising Association, tel: 0171 828 2771, mobile: 0385 224 815.

NOTES TO THE EDITOR

1. The Advertising Association is a federation of trade associations and professional bodies representing advertising, agencies, the media, and support services. It is the only body which speaks for all sides of an industry worth £12 billion.

2. Copies of the EU Commission's Green Paper on Commercial Communications in the Internal Market are available from the European Commission Office, 8 Storey's Gate, London, SW1P 3AT, tel: 0171 973 1992.

Figure 10.1 *Example of a well-produced news release*

NEWS **D/EE**

111/97

Department for
Education and Employment
21 May 1997

BLUNKETT CUTS RED TAPE

Education and Employment Secretary David Blunkett today promised teachers
the new Government would work with them to cut red tape and make more time to
raise standards.

At a summit meeting today with representatives from all six teacher unions Mr
Blunkett said:

"Whenever I meet teachers I hear cries to cut the bureaucracy to let us do our
jobs. Today I am announcing a working group with the task of cutting the bureaucratic
mountain and freeing teacher time to pursue our crusade to raise standards.

Press Enquiries: Charlotte Redman 0171 925 5105

Public Enquiries: 0171 925 5555

Figure 10.2 *Example of a news release from a government department: note details are given for further information*

the detail in the succeeding paragraphs and end with the least important point. Your news release can then be edited down with far less trouble.

Write in a factual style without flowery adjectives and superlatives when you are describing products and services. Avoid clichés, jargon words and comments as expressions of opinion. If you wish to make a comment about something, put it as a quote from someone in the organization. Just stick to the facts and let them stand on their own without embellishment. It will be up to the journalist to put his or her interpretation on the story you are issuing.

If there is a lot of technical data to be included put this as an attachment. Similarly, you can attach a verbatim speech, providing reference to it is made in the covering release.

Layout and style

The copy must be typed double-spaced. The reason for this is to give the sub-editor plenty of space to make changes.

NEWS RELEASE

RAILTRACK

PR97046
12 May 1997   Thameslink-1

EMBARGOED TO MONDAY 12 MAY 1997

THAMESLINK 2000 GOES PUBLIC

A six month public consultation programme for Railtrack's £580 million
Thameslink 2000 project was launched today.

Over the next six months over 60 local authorities in Greater London and
nine counties from Norfolk to West Sussex will be consulted about the proposal to
significantly increase capacity on the current Thameslink rail network.

For more information contact the Railtrack press office on 0171 344 7293/2.

PR97046
12 May 1997

Figure 10.3 *This Railtrack release follows all the rules*

Put at least a couple of lines between the heading and the first paragraph. Put extra space between paragraphs.

Do not underline any of the copy. This is the universal mark used by printers for copy to be set in italics. Do not set any of the text in italics or bold in the forlorn hope that it will be seen as more important. If a title of a book, film or article is used within the text, put it in single quotes.

Type on one side of the paper (white, A4) and if there is a continuation sheet, type 'More' at the foot of the page. Do not break a paragraph at the end of a page; if necessary take the whole paragraph over to the second page rather than leave a few words dangling (as a 'widow', the printer would say) at the top of the second page.

Leave a decent margin on each side, about 30mm (1¼ in). Do not try to achieve justified type when both sides are aligned. It is a waste of your time!

Use double quotes for direct quotations, (the actual words spoken); this is standard newspaper style. For reported speech follow the style in this extract from *The Times*: Eddie George *admitted* yesterday... he *suggested* there *were* some signs...

At the close of the copy, type END, or ENDS in capitals. If there are special points to be made for the attention of the editor, such as explanations of technical terms or how to obtain follow-up information, put these against a side-heading 'Note to Editor'. If possible, give a word count. This is usually easy to ascertain with reference to the spellcheck facility provided by most software packages. The sub-editor can then easily calculate the amount of space the copy will occupy when it is typeset.

Embargoes

Journalists dislike embargoes – which is a request to withhold publication until a specific time and date. Avoid them if possible, as they are not binding on the media and are there to give the journalist time for research or follow-up before a speech, or in advance of an announcement by a company or organization. If you decide to issue a release under embargo, make this clear above the title of the release. A suitable form of words would be.

EMBARGO: THIS INFORMATION IS ISSUED IN ADVANCE FOR YOUR CONVENIENCE. IT IS NOT FOR PUBLICATION, BROADCAST, OR USE ON CLUB TAPES BEFORE (time) ON (date).

The wording of embargoes for releases giving advance information on winners of awards requires care to ensure that details do not leak out in advance of the presentation event. An example is the wording for the Charter Mark Awards 1996 issued by the Office of Public Service, the Cabinet Office:

EMBARGO: THIS MATERIAL IS PROVIDED SO THAT RECIPIENTS MAY APPROACH THE NAMED CONTACTS IN ANY OF THE 1996 AWARD WINNING ORGANISATIONS FOR INFORMATION ABOUT THEIR WIN, PROVIDED THERE IS NO PUBLICATION OR PUBLICITY IN ANY MEDIA, ELECTRONIC OR WRITTEN, BEFORE 0001 HOURS GMT ON MONDAY 2 DECEMBER, 1996.

A simplified embargo notice can also be used so long as the restriction is absolutely clear and unambiguous. Take this example from a release issued by Hill and Knowlton (UK) on behalf of B&Q, the DIY retailer:

Press Information
EMBARGOED UNTIL 12.01am MONDAY 24 MARCH 1997.

Press Information
EMBARGOED UNTIL 12.01am MONDAY 24 MARCH 1997

EASTER SUNDAY STORE OPENING STILL A MYSTERY
TO EAST ANGLIAN SHOPPERS

Britain's leading DIY retailer, B&Q, has discovered that well over half of shoppers in East Anglia could be in for a frustrating experience on Easter Sunday. According to a survey conducted in the last few weeks, 61 per cent said they were unaware that the law prevents large retail outlets from trading on Easter Day, even though this is the third Easter since the trading legislation was introduced.

Figure 10.4 *A short embargo note for a release from Hill and Knowlton (UK)*

Issuing the release

Timing the release is fairly critical. If you are mailing it, don't forget that the post can take at least a day, and a release to a trade paper or magazine posted on a Friday night will not be seen until the following Monday morning. It's better to send it by messenger or to fax it, provided you are not sending photographs. E-mail is another possibility, but be aware that you are relying on someone to switch on their computer. A telephone call to the news desk saying a release is coming and will be on their screens (or has been sent) might help. Try it and if it works, use it regularly. But there is little to beat hard copy on paper.

WALKERS CRISPS KICKS OFF SCOTTISH SPORTING HEROES PROMOTION

Walkers Crisps is to launch its first ever Scottish instant win promotion, featuring Scotland's top ten sporting celebrities. Commencing on May 5th for eight weeks (see note 1), Walkers Sporting Heroes Promotion will offer school children and students the chance to win one of the ten top prizes of a training session with a Walkers Sporting Hero at their school.

Notes to editors:

1. The promotion will be launched in impulse outlets on May 5th and in grocery outlets on May 19th.

2. All winners must be aged 18 or under, and in full time education at a Scottish school in December 1997.

3. Ally McCoist is a centre forward for Rangers FC, Gavin Hastings has captained British Lions and Scotland rugby teams, Yvonne Murray is a 10,000 metre runner and is a Commonwealth champion, John Robertson is a centre forward for Heart of Midlothian FC, Jackie McNarmara is a wing back for Celtic FC and is a regular in Scotland's national team, Jim Leighton is a goalkeeper for Hibernian FC, Rob Wainwright is the current Scottish rugby captain, Derek Frame plays centre for City of Edinburgh and is also in the Scottish basketball team, Sandra Frame is a Scottish netball player and has competed in 3 World Championship and 2 World Games and Tony Hand is an ice hockey player and is acknowledged as the most talented UK born ice hockey player.

Issued on behalf of Walkers Snack Foods
For further information please contact:
Tara Byrne/Jackie Kelly
Hill & Knowlton (UK) Ltd
0171 413 3000   Date of issue: April 1997

Figure 10.5 *A release for a consumer product from Hill and Knowlton (UK)*

Is it news?

There is no point in sending out a news release if it is not news. You will only annoy the journalist if you do and your hard work will be wasted. So has your release got news value? The short answer is: does the news editor think it will interest the reader? News is something not known before.

To quote Pat Bowman, former head of public relations for Lloyds Bank:

News value is relative; minor stories make news on a slow day. Only big news counts on a busy day. A boring product story may be valuable news to a trade paper, but no publication with a general readership would look at it. How it is written will make all the difference in perception of a story: if it is written in a lively, interesting way it is more likely to be seen as important; if it is expressed in a boring fashion, using tedious, hard-to-grasp, waffly words and phrases then it will be considered dull. Then the only future for it is the waste bin.

Tabloids, says Bowman, are likely to be influenced by the entertainment and novelty value of a story, while the quality press will be more interested in stories that excite the intellect and imagination. Immediacy can also have an effect: it can outweigh importance in the assessment of news value, particularly for TV and radio. 'Don't try to bamboozle journalists into thinking that the story you are putting out is a good one when there is nothing new in it at all,' says Bowman. It could be an utter waste of time.

Robert Hornby's *The Press in Modern Society*, first published in 1965 but still relevant today, gives penetrating thoughts on news and news value. To summarize Hornby: what may appear as news in a provincial newspaper holding a dominant position in a city will bear little relationship in presentation to the same news splashed across the front page of a national daily. It is like comparing a seaside revue to a West End musical. So what are the basic elements of a news story? First, it must be something new. Other factors can be grouped under three headings – importance, human interest and topicality.

Importance can mean a well-known person connected with the story, perhaps a politician or public figure, especially if they have been in the news before.

Human interest is exemplified by something that is interesting to the many rather than the few. Anything pathetic, or that causes indignation, and the topics of prices, crime or abuse of privilege gets read. Other people's big financial gains, rags-to-

British Printing Industries Federation

Press Information

11 Bedford Row, London WC1R 4DX   Telephone 0171-242 6904   Facsimile 0171-405 7784

17th October 1996

NEW ECONOMIC SURVEY SHOWS IMPROVING PICTURE FOR PRINTING INDUSTRY

The first issue of *Directions*, the revamped and relaunched quarterly survey of economic trends from the British Printing Industries Federation, shows that printers are generally looking forward with confidence to the final quarter of the year, as the traditional seasonal uplift combines with cyclical economic recovery.

Directions is published quarterly by the British Printing Industries Federation.

Press release issued on behalf of the BPIF by AD Communications.

For further information contact John Howard or Emma Norgrove:-

Tel: 01372 464470
Fax: 01372 468626

Figure 10.6   *A trade association release giving detailed information for the trade press*

riches stories, romances, children, animal welfare, good/bad luck items, the unexpected, the surprising and the unusual always attract attention. Most people prefer reading about people to things: many column inches of publicity can easily be lost if releases ignore the human angle.

Journalists' requirements are changing in line with the instant delivery of news on television and radio. In consequence, newspapers are increasingly filling their pages with background stories and feature articles on such subjects as lifestyles, health, entertainment, sport, home and garden. These subjects are all fertile ground for human interest stories.

Topicality means facts about a subject of intense current interest, with excitement, danger and rapid movement (like chases and police hunts); well-known faces must be photographed in easily recognized places and backgrounds to provide maximum impact and make for easy recognition. A great deal of the trivial derives its news value from such topicality, especially in the popular press.

Study newspaper style

Look at newspapers to see how journalists write: whether broadsheet or tabloid, extremes of style determine the way different newspapers approach a given story. The former will probably give far more detail, while the latter will tend to over-simplify, leaving little room for intelligent interpretation.

Write to catch the eye of the reader in the same way as the journalist does. One thing is certain: a 'new' story or one that has not been published before has got news value; and if it is exclusive it will have an even better chance of publication.

No puffs please

Releases must not become blatant advertising messages on behalf of the client company or other organizations. If you put out an advertisement under the guise of a news story it is sure to put the editor off and ruin your reputation as a public relations professional into the bargain.

These so-called 'puffs', which attempt to gain editorial space, should properly be paid-up advertisements. But a new product or service can of course be a news story for release to the specialist press covering the industry sector you are covering.

Releases to the specialist press

If you write a release containing technical matter there is no profit in using jargon meaningless to the average reader, or writing in a highbrow way to woo white-coated boffins.

Marion Clarke, corporate communications manager of Pira International, the Surrey-based printing research and technology organization, has considerable experience in this area. 'Our releases are mostly on technical subjects but if they are written in

Press release

Pira International
Randalls Road
Leatherhead
Surrey KT22 7RU
United Kingdom

Telephone
Leatherhead (code UK-44) 01372 802000

Fax
Leatherhead (code UK-44) 01372 802238

9739

June 1997

(532 words)

**New report predicts continued price uncertainity
for global pulp and paper industry**

Figure 10.7 *The writer of this release has the sub-editor in mind:
note the number of words has a prominent position*

simple, concise language, only using scientific terms when
absolutely necessary, then they are usually used word for
word,'she says. Few technical journalists are specialists and fully
trained in the technologies they write about. If you provide copy
that needs little editing your release is far less likely to be
changed than if you give them gobbledygook, however well
intentioned that may be.

Don't forget the Internet

Most large companies and organizations now make their press
releases available on the Internet. For example, BT in their
'Let's Talk' page direct the user to their News Releases from
which all releases issued since 1995, month by month, can be
seen and printed out if required. Leading organizations in the
communications field, such as The Institute of Public Relations,
the Institute of Practitioners in Advertising, the Advertising
Association and many of the national media organizations all
have Internet sites from which their press releases can be
downloaded. Again, it is important that contact names and day/
night telephone numbers are included, as well as background
information.

Commissioned articles

If you are asked to write an article by a newspaper or magazine, or if you put up an idea for a feature, the content and prime thrust of the piece should be discussed with the editor well in advance. The brief subsequently agreed must be scrupulously followed. If it diverts, then it is likely that the editor will ask for amendments some of which may be substantial. Worse than that, changes may be made that you know nothing about until the article is printed – and then it is too late!

Write in the style of the publication and keep to the number of words requested. Nothing is more annoying for an editor if the article is well over the length specified and won't fit into the space allotted for it. If that happens, then your copy will be cut, and that may defeat your objectives. Similarly, if you commission someone else in the organization to write the article, then be sure that the brief is followed, even if you have to exert some persuasion.

Don't forget to include illustrations. Most editors will require photographs, drawings, graphs or tables to support the points you are making or just to catch the reader's eye. Give the piece a title and put the author's name – the by-line – underneath. Make sure the article has shape: a beginning, a middle and an end. And if you type the number of words at the end, the editor will be a friend for life. But above all, keep to the deadline!

11

Captions: how to handle them

Always provide captions for any photographs or illustrations accompanying news releases; these are used extensively in company annual reports and brochures. Care is essential in their preparation and handling: too often captions are left to the end, with the result that the caption lets down the illustration and the news story or article.

The important point about captions is that they lead the reader to the body copy. They provide an instant point of interest and will often turn a magazine 'page flipper' into a reader. Much thought should go into how a caption is written and presented, for if it misleads or contains errors, the communication can be irreparably spoilt.

Photo captions with releases

The caption to a photograph or illustration either accompanying a news release or sent separately as a caption story, is as important as the picture itself. If it fails to describe the person, product or service, all the effort and cost involved can be wasted. It can turn into a public relations disaster waiting to happen: once the photograph with its caption has left your hands there is little you can do to put matters right if you have misnamed someone or misspelt their name.

Only when the picture is published do you realize that you have made a mistake – you go hot all over – but by then the damage is done. Although you may know who the people are in a picture, others may not, and will rely on you to tell them!

Caption content and style

Captions should be brief, certainly not exceeding 50 to 60 words, and reveal the content of the photo. Put a heading, typed double spaced, and give the name of the issuing organization, company or consultancy with date, contact name, address and telephone/fax numbers. Refer to the source organization, service or product.

If the photo shows a person or group of people, put job titles and names from left to right. When a well-known personality is featured, write the caption round the VIP, not someone else, even if you feel you ought to mention the chairman first! Photographic prints are expensive – black and white glossies cost anything from £5, colour prints twice that – so take care that the caption does justice to the story.

Captions for the press

Always use a stiff-backed envelope when sending out photographs or illustrations. Do not write on the back of prints as Biro or pencil marks can show through and make the picture useless for reproduction. Captions should be attached with strips of Sellotape. Never glue or paste them to the backs of photographs; just stick them on lightly so they protrude from the bottom of the print and can be read in conjunction with the picture.

Copyright issues

When you send out photographs to the press, always be aware of the copyright issue. News editors and picture desks will assume that photographs received from public relations people, especially when they accompany a release, will be free of copyright restrictions.

Photographs should be rubber-stamped on the back with a statement of the copyright position; ideally, similar wording should appear on the caption itself. Never issue a photograph or illustration unless you are sure who owns the copyright. (The owner of the copyright is the author or creator – see the Institute of Public Relations guideline paper *Public Relations and the Law*.)

Captions in publications

Clear, concise captioning is the hallmark of a well-produced, stylish publication. In many cases, particularly with annual reports, shareholders get no further than the pictures. One way of getting the reader to take notice of the text is to have an arresting photograph with the caption leading on to a particular point.

Distinguishing captions from text

Set off captions from the text by using smaller type, different typeface, or by setting in italics or bold if the text is in plain or roman type. You can position captions in the margin, away from the bulk of the text. Sometimes it is possible to reverse out the caption on a photograph if there is a sufficiently dark area. There is a danger of the caption being unreadable if it is reversed out of a light toned part of the picture.

An effective way to make captions stand out from the text is to print them in a second colour, preferably using one of the colours chosen for corporate house style. But take care that the colour is a strong one: if it is a pastel shade then the wording will be lost on white paper! If you set two- or three-word headings as intros to captions then you give added visual impact.

Always describe the picture or drawing, unless it is purely for decoration. State essential details, but not what the eye can see for itself. If it is an action shot say what is happening. Even if you think it is obvious, it might not be so to the reader. It is infuriating, for instance, to see an interesting photograph featuring a new product and management team, and not know what it illustrates or who the people are. Don't forget that a wrongly named person could mean a furious client, possibly a reprint, or even – horror of horrors – a libel action.

Lure the reader to the text

The caption should arrest attention and lure the reader to the text unless the photograph or illustration is there just to brighten up the page and not meant to tell a story in itself. Write crisply; you don't want just a 'label' making a bland, boring statement.

The caption might be read and understood while the text may not: the reader may not get as far as that! Make sure it contains a verb, preferably in the present tense, and if possible some news value. Journalists often get stories from the captions in annual reports, and from house journals and brochures.

Captions for charts

The chart caption should describe the essential finding or purpose and lead the reader to the relevant part of the text. With graphs and tables ensure that legends and headings are clear and unambiguous. Make sure that graph axes are explained and show the appropriate units.

Captioning groups of photographs

When you have several photographs or illustrations to caption, arrange the captions together in a block and number them. If there are several photographs of people, it is convenient to have an outline line drawing showing people's positions with a numbered key for identification.

Take time and trouble in the wording and presentation of captions. Increased readership and improved communication will inevitably result.

12

Office style

Good, consistent style is just as important for correspondence, forms of address, wording for invitations and correct use of courtesy titles, as it is for publications and other printed matter. Good style is good manners, and that means answering – or at least acknowledging – letters no later than two or three days following receipt, and returning telephone calls where possible the same day.

Presentation and layout are also key factors in getting your message across. Every letter, report, paper or printed invitation that goes out must reflect the style and corporate image of your organization. If it is not up to standard or specification, then your public relations effort could well be wasted. If there is no set house style, then now is the time to establish rules for everyone in the office to follow.

Suggested style for correspondence

Most firms and organizations have style rules for letters, envelopes and other office stationery such as invoices, order forms, fax messages and internal memos. A properly addressed and signed-off letter is the first point. Here are some of the basics.

Layout

File reference and date should be ranged left and aligned with an element of the letterhead design. Do not put full stops, commas or other punctuation in addresses typed at the top of the letter. The following specimen layout style is commonplace:

Mr John Smith
123 Any Road
Anytown
Kent AN5 1ZZ

When addresses are set in a line, say in the body of a letter, then commas are used to separate the components as in Mr John Smith, 123 Any Road, Anytown, Kent AN5 1ZZ.

Courtesy titles

Titles at tops of letters and salutations are normally Mr/Mrs/Miss/Ms. When answering the telephone do not just say 'Hello' or even the modern but overused and insincere response 'This is Mandy, how can I help you?' Give just your surname or add your Christian name if you want. Do not give yourself a courtesy title and say 'This is *Mr* Smith speaking.'

It is worth noting that the abbreviation *Ms* is now under threat from a new generation of women who feel it is outdated and smacks of aggressive feminism. According to a report in the *Sunday Times*, March 1997, the UK Federation of Professional Women want *Ms* replaced by the single prefix *Miss* for all women, married or single. So it seems that *Ms* is slowly dying a death not only here but in the USA where it is believed to have originated.

Honours and qualifications

Where style calls for the inclusion of designations such as civil honours and qualifications, these should follow the established abbreviations, ie, MBE, BA, BSc. No stops go between characters or after separate designations.

Dates

Separate the day of the week from the month: *2 April 1997*. If the day goes after the month then it collides with the year and can look messy. Avoid *nd/st/rd/th* after the day numeral. When referring to times of day, type these with no space between the figures and *am/pm* as in 9am, 9.30am. Do not put noughts after the figure: for instance 9.00 am would look cluttered and pedantic. The signee's name should be ranged left with the person's title typed underneath when needed. Do not underline the name or title, or put either in capitals. Use a fountain pen to sign letters, not a Biro or felt-tip.

Copies

Where copies of the letter are sent outside the organization, the addressee's name should appear beneath the signature, ranged left as in:

Copy to: Mr John Smith, XYZ Company.

Details on people receiving blind copies, where the name(s) is not disclosed to the addressee, should ideally appear in a different position.

Letterheads

These should be printed in the same typeface, colour and style as all other in-house stationery. Postal address, telephone, facsimile and e-mail addresses and, if appropriate, the world wide web site address should all be shown in a prominent position. Public relations department headings should carry, where appropriate, out-of-hours telephone numbers, although many firms will prefer to show this information separately rather than have it printed with the heading.

Other stationery

Style for invoices, statements, order forms, fax messages, envelopes and other printed stationery should all follow the house style with logo (if there is one), and typefaces and colour identical to those used for letterheads. Infinite variations in size are possible with computer-controlled typesetting systems. Your printer and designer will advise on how these can be employed to the best advantage from both a design and cost point of view.

Have clear clean layout

If the layout of reports and documents has been well designed, then the message and information contained is more likely to be communicated and acted upon. The basic requirement for an effective layout is a legible typeface, following house style, and preferably the same as the one used for correspondence. If the typeface for correspondence is used for all stationery, and a uniform style of headings and subheadings is adopted, then all paperwork is immediately identified with the organization. If it can follow the style for printwork as well, so much the better.

A distinctive 'look' to your correspondence and reports will be achieved if basic style is followed: width of margins, number of words per page, page size, uniform space between the lines (leading), type and weight of paper. Put a little extra space between paragraphs, but do not try to squeeze too many lines into one page. Do not use italics or bold type within the body copy in an attempt to give added emphasis.

Forms of address

Public relations people often have to decide how to begin and end a letter to royalty, and how to address government ministers, peers, MPs and civic dignitaries. Bad form – or at least insensitivity to tradition – can mean that your invitation to give a keynote speech or perform an opening ceremony will lead to a frosty reply. Care in addressing everyone with whom you are in contact, not just VIPs, is essential.

The British system of titles, forms of address and precedence is one of the most complicated in the western world. Nevertheless, most – if not all – answers are to be found in *Debrett's Correct Form*, which covers every conceivable situation in correspondence and in sending invitations to social and business functions. A few examples may be helpful to the reader, but for full guidance refer to Debrett's.

Writing to firms

When writing to firms, avoid 'Dear Sir/Madam'. When you do not have a name – it is usually easy to find it in telephone or trade directories – address your letter to the position, ie to the chairman, managing director or secretary. When writing to the press, write Dear Editor if you do not know his or her name. But it is always worth the trouble to write personally if you can, although a name on the envelope and letter will seldom ensure a reply or even an acceptance!

Royalty

When writing to the Sovereign, all communications should be addressed to The Private Secretary to The Queen, to the office holder rather than by name, unless you know the person. For other members of the Royal Family, write to the Equerry, Private Secretary or Lady in Waiting as appropriate, the letter beginning Dear Sir or Dear Madam, again to the holder of the office rather than by name. In direct communications, start with Dear Sir or Dear Madam with 'Your Royal Highness' substituted for 'you' and 'Your Royal Highness's' for 'your' in the body of the letter.

Peerage

When writing to the peerage, put (for example) 'My Lord Duke' in the formal form and 'Dear Duke' in the informal, or the 'Duke of —' if the acquaintanceship is slight. Verbal address is 'Your Grace' (formal), 'Duke' (social). Special styles are accorded to the wives and children of peers.

Baronets

With baronets, letters begin 'Dear Sir John' (for example) with Bt added on the envelope. A similar style applies for knighthoods where the title is held for life, but the surname should be added if you do not know the person well. Should you meet a baronet or knight in the street or at a function, he should be addressed as Sir John, never 'Sir' on its own. The wife of a baronet or knight is known as 'Lady' followed by the surname.

Government ministers

Ministers of cabinet rank and some other junior ministers are members of the Privy Council and have the prefix The Rt Hon before their names, with the letters PC after all honours and decorations awarded by the Crown. Privy Counsellors (the preferred spelling) are drawn from many other areas of public life, so watch out! Addressing letters to government ministers is straightforward: Dear Sir (or Madam) for the formal style, Mrs or Miss for the informal with the option of Dear Minister when writing by his/her appointment.

Members of Parliament

Unless MPs are Privy Counsellors, they have just MP after their name plus any civil or military honours. They are addressed Mr/Mrs/Miss in the usual way. Members of the House of Commons do not have MP after their name once they lose their seat. Always check with the current edition of *Vacher's Parliamentary Companion, PMS Parliamentary Companion* or other reference source when writing to MPs and members of the House of

Lords. These publications also include details of ministers and senior civil servants in Departments of State, and the names of officials in other government departments and agencies.

Civic dignitaries

There are widely differing styles for civic dignitaries, depending on the particular town or city. The Lord Mayors of London and York are unique in that they are styled 'The Right Honourable' while the remainder are generally titled 'The Right Worshipful'. They are addressed at the beginning of a letter 'My Lord Mayor' and the envelope should bear the wording 'The Right Honourable the Lord Mayor of —' Mayors of cities and towns are addressed 'Mr Mayor' and the envelope should carry the words 'The Right Worshipful the Mayor of (City of)/(Royal Borough of)' or 'The Worshipful The Mayor of —' Letters should be signed off 'Yours faithfully' (or Yours sincerely if a social occasion).

Debrett's should be consulted for checking titles of church dignitaries, officers in the armed forces, ambassadors, and for deciding precedence for table plans and guest lists.

Invitations to functions

Printed invitation cards should be sent for most functions, although in many cases – say for press conferences and for informal or social events – a well presented letter will suffice. Gold-edged cards are best and use of a script typeface is particularly suitable for formal occasions. The card must state the name (or office) of the person making the invitation, the nature of the function, where it will be held, the date and time and the dress. It should also state if decorations should be worn. The card must provide enough space for the name of the invitee, and an RSVP name and address, plus telephone number if appropriate. If possible, provide a prepaid reply card. The invitee's name should be handwritten in black ink.

Replies to invitations

Replies should be sent out on the organization's usual printed letterheads and ideally be written in the formal style, stating either acceptance of the invitation or regret at being unable to accept. State the reason for non-acceptance, examples being 'owing to a previous engagement/absence abroad/out of town that day'. Whether accepting or declining, the name(s) of the invitee(s) should be given, together with details of the function. If replying by telephone, send a written follow-up.

Acknowledging correspondence

Good style means good manners. And good manners is good PR. Nothing is worse than not replying to a letter. It is usually possible to send a reply within a day or two. If you are too busy to post a typed letter, then a handwritten one will do just as well, even if you have to handwrite the envelope yourself.

An acknowledgement card is also helpful and should be sent as a matter of routine for all correspondence where a detailed and immediate response is not possible. This might simply state '(name of person of company/organization) thanks you for your communication of (date) and is receiving attention'. It takes only a minute or two of your time to get off a reply of some sort: a telephone call or faxed note will often do the trick.

Setting out documents

The layout for reports, documents, agendas and minutes calls for a consistent and well-ordered style. A printed heading should give the name, address and telephone/fax numbers of the organization on all documents. Date and reference numbers to aid identification should be included. Insert extra space between items and leave generous margins (at least 25mm on the right-hand margin, more on the left). Call in a professional designer to give you a template for word processor operators to follow. That way everybody will produce documents to a consistent style, an essential requirement for developing a recognizable corporate image.

Writing a cv

Style for presentation of a curriculum vitae (cv) is important and could affect an applicant's chances of securing employment. It should be clear and concise, consistent in style, accurate without spelling errors or wrong punctuation, use plain English and should concentrate on skills and achievements. A cv must be typewritten or word-processed on two sheets of plain white A4 paper, with plenty of space so that the words and headings are not jammed up tight. Always address the cv to a named person, never Dear Sir or Dear Madam. It only takes a minute or two to find the right name. Do not use coloured paper or ink and pay particular attention to the way it is laid out. It could mean all the difference to getting the job or not.

A cv should provide the following information: name, address, date of birth, marital status, nationality, education and qualifications, career history and the names of two referees.

There are numerous books on preparing a cv, *The Jobsearch Manual* by Linda Apsey being particularly suitable for younger people starting out on their careers. *Super Jobsearch* by Peter K Studner is appropriate for those seeking management positions. Both are published by Management Books 2000.

13

Traps, snares and pitfalls

Appropriate choice of words is of paramount importance for imparting the sense and tone of any message. But for that message to be properly understood, and for it to be clear and unambiguous, not only must spellings be correct but the writer must avoid slang in formal texts, guard against overusing fashionable but sloppy phrases, and know whether words are hyphenated or not, or spelt as one word. This chapter examines some of these traps which can lead to mistakes or even howlers which make your hair stand on end when you see them in print.

Spelling points

Difficulty often arises with advis*or* or advis*er*: the preferred spelling is *-er*; *-or* is pretentious, even old-fashioned. A useful rule is that unless preceded by a 't' or 'ss' verb (or less frequently noun) endings are usually *-er*. In order to avoid a spelling hiccup (not *hiccough* nowadays) you have to be on guard for mistakes like *practioners* – or literals and typos as printers like to call them. There is no 'd' in *allege*, it is *contractual*, not *-ural*, *flotation* not *floatation, hurrah/hurray* not *hoorah/ay* unless you are talking about a *Hooray Henry; idiosyncrasy* not *-acy; minuscule* not *-iscule; nerve racking*, not *-wracking*. It is a *gentlemen's agreement*, not *-man's*.

Confusion often occurs between *passed* and *past*. The past tense and past participle of the verb to pass is *passed* as in *it passed from you to me*, whereas *past* as an adjective describes things or events that have occurred (*past times*); it can also be a preposition as in *first past the post* and a noun (*memories of the past*).

For words of more than one syllable ending in *-ed* or *-ing* and with the stress on the last syllable, the final consonant is doubled as in *permit/permitted*. But where the last syllable is unstressed, as in *target* and *focus* the final consonant is not doubled: thus any argument on how to spell *focused/focusing* and *targeted/targeting* is instantly resolved. In the same category go other favourite words in the PR vocabulary such as *benefited/ing, budgeted/ing*. Another way of telling whether you are right or wrong is to pronounce such words with a stressed doubled final consonant and so get fo*cuss*ed and tar*gett*ed. Or say to yourself mar*kett*ing, with a double 't' and the emphasis on the second syllable; it is obviously wrong and you will instantly recall the rule. (Get into the habit of looking out for a double 's' or 't' in these words – you won't have to wait long!)

With suffixes of words ending in a single 'l', the last consonant is usually doubled whether or not the final syllable is stressed as in *labelled/travelled*, but note *appealed/paralleled*.

Spellings of similar sounding or pairs of words frequently cause trouble. Take these examples: *canvas* (to cover with) but *canvass* (solicit votes); *dependant* (relative) but *dependent* (upon). How many times have you seen these words misused and misspelt? Then there is the *draughtsman* (of a specification) but someone who *drafts* a document, the official who makes a formal *inquiry*, but a person who questions and makes an *enquiry*. *Further* has quite a different meaning from *farther*: the former suggests something additional to say or do, the latter increased distance.

Install becomes installation but *instalment* (sometimes with a double 'l'), all three having a totally different meaning to *instil.* A common mistake is to mix up *licence* (noun) with *license* (verb): how many times do you want to tell a shopkeeper to correct *licenced* to *licensed?* (In America, it is the other way round and 'practice' is both noun and verb.)

How often have you asked someone whether the first 'e' should be dropped in *judgement?* The rule here is that when a suffix beginning with a consonant (*-ful, -ling,-ly, -ment, -ness, -some*) is added to a word with a silent 'e', the -e is retained – but not always (exceptions include *argument, fledgling*). *Judgement* usually loses the first 'e' in legal works. In American spelling, the 'e' is dropped before a suffix beginning with a consonant as in *abridgment, judgment.* Another rule worth noting is when adding *in-* and *un-* to the beginning of a word; there is only one 'n' unless the word itself begins with an 'n' as in *inseparable, unending, innumerable, unnecessary.*

Other confusing spellings are *principle* (basis of reasoning) and *principal* (main); *stationary* (still) and *stationery* (paper stocks) – a way to remember this is 'e' for envelope. Note that the start of the last syllable in *supersede* and *consensus* is often misspelt with a 'c'. Keep a *colander* for straining and a *calendar* for giving the date; reserve *program* and *disk* for computer terminology, and resist the temptation to put an 'e' in *whisky* (whiskey is for the American and Irish, but never Scotch whisky – the Scots wouldn't hear of it!).

Use your dictionary

It is difficult to remember different spellings for similar-sounding words, but being aware of the similarities and possible spelling errors encourages the writer to reach for the dictionary.

Before leaving the subject of spellings, one sure tip is always remember to use the computer's spellcheck for everything – releases, articles, reports and letters; not only will it pick up errors that might otherwise not be noticed, it will often provide a word count by recording the number of questionable words. This is extremely useful information for both the writer and editor, saving the tiresome task of counting up copy word by word to estimate the length when set in type. More examples are in Appendix 2.

-ise or -ize verb endings

Both spellings are common in the UK, while the *-ize* ending is usual in North America. There are some word-s which must always end with *-ise*: *advertise/advise/televise*, for example. Few style gurus will object to *-ise* throughout, although the use of *capsize/sterilize/familiarize* will seldom be criticized. In the UK until a few years ago *-ize* endings were commonly seen in *The Times* and elsewhere, but as both the Oxford University Press and the Cambridge University Press switched to *-ise*, so newspapers tended to follow suit and thus another style trend was born. Even so, *-ize* appears to be as firmly embedded in America as ever. However much you may hate nouns becoming verbs, you have to realize that services are *privatized*, but most of us will object to being *hospitalized* or having plans *prioritized*.

One word or two?

Many words once happily hyphenated, or some two-word phrases, soon found themselves living together, joined without remorse. Thus we have seen *railwayman/paybed/turnout* enter everyday usage as examples of lost hyphenation. Many still persist in using *alright* ('Gross, coarse, crass and to be avoided', says Kingsley Amis in *The King's English*) instead of the preferred *all right*.

The American tendency to write *underway* as one word has few followers here. But who is to say that it is no different from *anyway*. Then there is the frequent confusion between *forever* (perpetually) and *for ever* (for always), as in 'He is *forever* complaining' against 'He will be in the same firm *for ever*.' Amis again: '*I'm forever blowing bubbles* to be outlawed altogether.' But few will condone the modern trend for *anymore* or *anytime* which cry out for their original two-word forms.

Many hyphenated words eventually end up as one for the simple reason that the style is modern and favoured by the popular press. We are used to them and no longer worry whether they are hyphenated or not. However, it is advisable to check with the usual reference sources such as the *Oxford English Dictionary* for recommended style for individual word-sets.

Puzzles and posers

When you *accede* to something you give assent to an opinion or policy; do not use it to mean *grant, allow, agree*. Rather than write *accordingly*, put *so* or *therefore*; adverbs like *hopefully, admittedly, happily* are usually unnecessary. It is better to write you *plan* or *intend* to do something than *hope to do it, which* suggests doubt that it will ever be done. Rather than *adjust* something, *change* it; you *appraise* it when you judge its value, not *apprise* which means inform.

Among is often confused with *between*. When writing about more than two things or people, *among* is usually needed. But when considered individually, *between* is preferred. Contrast 'food was shared *among* six people' with 'cordial relations *between* the UK, France and Germany'.

Avoid hackneyed words like *factor* which can usually be omitted without loss of sense. You can dispense with it easily, for example, 'in an important *factor* in the company's success' by recasting and writing simply 'important in the company's success'. *Feature* (as a noun) is another word that adds nothing and can easily be dropped. *Meaningful* has lost all meaning and is another candidate for excision. Also cut out *one of the most, respective/respectively, currently, the foreseeable future, the fact is...* and other words that contribute little except waffle.

Don't be old fashioned and write *amongst* and *whilst* when *among* and *while* do just as well. You should *try to* do something, not *try and* do it. Instead of writing *practically* all the time put *almost, nearly*, or *all but*. The world is populated by *people*, not *persons*; but that is not to say that there is no place for *person*. The noun *person* is normally only used in the singular as in 'he was a *person* of character'. Avoid using *persons* when *people* would be more appropriate.

Be careful not to add a qualifier to ungradable words like *unique* or *perfect*. You cannot have degrees of uniqueness or perfection: either something is unique or perfect or it is not. Other words like this are *peculiar, sole, single, spontaneous*.

Watch out for *get/got*. While there is nothing actually wrong with them, they appear informal and should be avoided. Use *obtain* or *possess* instead, or consider rewriting. Also take care with *to lay, to lie*: the verb *to lay* takes an object while *to lie* does not (I *lay* my body on the floor as I *lie* resting). But you never have *a lay down* which makes a noun of it!

Like is another pitfall. Used parenthetically, to qualify a following or preceding statement, as in '*like* I was going to tell you something' is a vulgarism of the first order, Fowler says. But resistance to its use as a conjunction and as a substitute for *as if* or *as though* is crumbling.

Keep clear of *nice* (a favourite with women). Fowler says: 'It should be confined in print to dialogue... ladies have charmed it out of all its individuality and converted it into a mere diffuser of vague and mild agreeableness.' It is better to forget *nice* and choose a synonym for it, unless you are in America and use the catchphrase 'Have a *nice* day.'

Arguments abound on whether to write (or say) *compared to* or *compared with*. The first is to liken one thing to another as in 'I prefer apples compared *to*,' while the second points to differences or resemblances between two things as in 'comparing the speaker's notes *with* what has been written'. Use *different from* in writing, keep *different to* for speech.

Avoid imprecisions such as *lots of, many* or *things* when figures or definitions can be given. Keep *an* for words beginning with a silent 'h' (*an heir, an honour, an honorarium*); otherwise it is *a hotel, a harbour, a hero, a hope*. Introduce a list of items with *such as* or *for example*, not *etc.*

Note that *anybody* and *anyone* are singular (*anybody* is able to visit the museum), as are *every, everybody, everyone* (*every* dentist *has* information on care of teeth; *everybody* is able to discuss *his* or *her* problems with a lawyer). *Each* is singular (*each* contributor should check *his* or *her* paper), and so is *nobody* or *no one* (no one is certain).

Vogue words and phrases

Numerous words are not only overused or become clichés but suggest the writer has not bothered to think of anything better. Top of the list must be *or whatever* when it means in effect 'including many other things'. Don't say it and certainly never write it.

Then there are the clichés of *having said that, at the end of the day, in-depth, ongoing and ongoing situation, geared to, in terms of, I'll get back to you, name of the game, no problem, take on board, track record*; and words like *feedback, concept, consensus, lifestyle, viable, syndrome, validate, interface*. Some, if not all of these words are current coinage in the communications industry and it is virtually impossible to avoid them. Try to find synonyms.

Getting in the mood

If you fail to distinguish between auxiliary (modal) verbs and between relative pronouns, verbal inelegances and even mistakes arise. While sometimes interchangeable without loss of sense, look out for pitfalls. Here are a few examples.

Modal verbs *shall/will, should/could, can/could, may/might* each possess different shades of meaning, expressed as moods or modes of action. Also within this category are *must* and *ought*.

Unlike ordinary verbs, modals do not have *-s* or *-ed* added in present and past tenses; there can be no *shalls, mighting* or *oughted* apart from being *willed* to do something.

The general rule is that *shall* and *should* go with first person singular and plural; *will* and *would* the others. Thus, *should* accompanies *I* and *we*; and *would goes* with *he, she, it* and *they*. Both express simple future tense; *will* showing intention or determination, especially a promise to do something. You are more likely to be taken seriously if you say 'I *will* be in the office on Sunday.' '*Shall be*' somewhat dilutes the intention.

Care is needed in choosing *should* or *would* for there is a subtle but important difference between them. *Should* has moral force behind it, whereas *would* acquires mild conditionality. *Should* expresses three future possibilities: conditional, probable, and a less likely outcome as in, respectively, 'I *should* be grateful if you *would* answer my letter'; 'she *should* avoid the angry client'; '*should* you see him, remind him about the meeting.' *Could*, like *should/would*, indicates a conditional or future possibility, while *could/can*, used interrogatively, suggests seeking permission.

Difficulty often occurs in using *may/might*. Permission is expressed through *may* as in '*may I*', but both imply simple possibility in 'the client *may/might* come' and are indistinguishable. In some contexts *might* hints at uncertainty and suggests less optimism than *may* as in 'they *might* use the release' against 'they *may* be able to edit it'. Thus, *may/might* are often interchangeable where the truth of an event is unknown, but if there is no longer uncertainty, use *might*.

James Aitchison in his *Guide to Written English* neatly expresses *ought* and *must* as 'duty, obligation and necessity'; *ought*, he observes, suggests likelihood of fulfilment, while *must* indicates strict or absolute necessity.

Another trap can arise in writing *which* and *that*. These pronouns are normally used with non-human nouns, otherwise write *who* or *whom*. While *which/that* can often be interchanged or even omitted without loss of sense, distinctions exist, particularly when sub-clauses beginning *which* are enclosed in commas. It is rare to punctuate *that* clauses in the same way. *That* defines, *which* informs.

It is a sound rule (says Sir Ernest Gowers in *The Complete Plain Words*) that *that* should be dispensed with whenever this can be done 'without loss of clarity or dignity'. Consult the *Oxford Guide to English Usage* or Fowler for examples of current *which/that* usage.

Genteelisms

Substitution of a normal, natural word for another that is considered by some as less familiar, less vulgar, less improper or less apt is defined by Fowler as a genteelism. For instance, *assist* for help, *ale* for beer, *endeavour* for try, *odour* for smell are all genteelisms, along with *ladies* for women and *gentlemen* for men. A word that is simple and unpretentious is to be preferred to one that has a high-sounding, euphemistic ring to it. Words that were once listed as genteelisms (*chiropodist* for corn-cutter for example) have long since gained acceptance for everyday usage, and are no longer indicators of social class.

Here is a short but easily extendible list of other genteelisms for you to be aware of and preferably avoid: euphemisms such as *conceal* for hide, *corpulent* for fat, *ere* for before, *demise* or *passed away* for died, *dentures* for false teeth, *donation* for gift, *lounge* for sitting-room, *perspire* for sweat, *retire* for go to bed, *reside at* for live at, *sufficient* for enough, *take umbrage* for take offence, *toilet* for lavatory. And so on.

Keep clear of slang

Unless part of a direct quotation, say in a speech delivered at an event other than an AGM, avoid slang words in formal writing. But you need to appreciate that today's slang is tomorrow's idiom. Slang words for 'publicize', drawn from the *Wordsworth Thesaurus of Slang* include the following: *promote, hype, plug, push, pitch, splash, spot, boost, build up, puff, ballyhoo, beat the drum for, tub-thump, hard/soft sell.* If you are a publicity seeker, you are a *hot dogger, publicity hound, showoff.* Slang for 'publicity' includes *hoopla, flack, flackery, big noise, ink, get ink.*

While *state of the art and cutting edge* began as slang, these phrases have now found a place in the everyday language of communicators. Doubtless, many other spoken slang words will eventually find a final resting place in formal writing.

14

The spoken word: pronunciation matters

The way words are spoken is just as important as the way they are written. Well enunciated speech, pronounced according to established guidelines, can help platform performance, aid communication between an organization and its audience and make a significant contribution to the public relations effort.

Corporate image is not just the logo and visual impact of literature – the typeface, colours and house style. Much also depends on word of mouth and the mental picture of the speaker that is built up by tone of voice. And that picture is the one which can make all the difference between success and failure at a client presentation, a shareholders' meeting, a conference speech, or even a job interview.

No one wants to hear slipshod, careless speech like 'See yer layer', dropped or wrongly stressed vowels and syllables, missed consonants, a high-speed mumbo-jumbo of words shortened to the extent that they become almost unintelligible. Here are some basic points of pronunciation and some verbal mishaps that are so easily made, but seldom corrected.

Received Pronunciation

Among the many varieties of English, Received Pronunciation (RP) is the standard most dictionaries follow. This is said to be 'the least regional being originally that used by educated speakers in southern England' (*OED*), and the *Oxford Guide to English Usage* takes it as 'the neutral national standard, just as it is in its use in broadcasting or in the teaching of English as a foreign language'. The new edition of *Fowler's Modern English Usage* makes specific recommendations based on RP and the pronunciations given are largely those of the *Oxford Concise English Dictionary (COD)*. It is from these, and other sources such as the BBC guide *The Spoken Word*, that examples have been taken of pronunciation where uncertainty exists.

It is useful to differentiate between pronunciation and accent. As Kingsley Amis points out in *The King's English* 'everyone's *accent* [his italics] is a general thing that depends roughly on a speaker's place of birth, upbringing, education and subsequent environment whereas *pronunciation* is a question of how individual words are spoken'. It can thus be deduced that pronunciation of a given word can be considered 'correct' while another may be 'incorrect'. RP provides a useful but limited yardstick by which pronunciation may be judged correct or not.

One of the most argued points is the placing of stress. If you know where it falls, the pronunciation of vowels can be determined. Look for the stress accent ´ (like the French acute) after the stressed syllable or vowel sound which is shown in almost every word in the *COD* and in most popular dictionaries, even the well-thumbed pocket editions to be found in most office drawers. The stressed syllable (or vowel) is italicized in the following examples.

RP speakers will put the stress first in *ad*ult, *app*licable, *con*troversy, *comm*unal, *bro*chure, *in*tegral, *form*idable, *kil*ometre, *mis*chievous, *pa*tent (*pay*-tent), *pref*erable, *prim*arily, *rep*utable, *temp*orarily; but second in ba*nal*, con*trib*ute, demon-strable, dis*pute*, dis*trib*ute, re*search*, trans*fer*able. *Int*eresting loses the second syllable to become *intr*'sting. Stress on the third syllable occurs with app*a*ratus (as in *hate*), compos*i*te (as in *opposite*, inter*ne*cine as in *knee*).

Make sure there is not an intrusive 'r' in *drawing room* (not draw-ring), *an idea of* (not idea-r-of). Avoid the American habit of stressing -ar in *nec*essarily (not necess*a*rily) and *temp*orarily (not tempor*a*rily).

While 'h' is silent in *hour*, it is aspirated in *hotel* and so therefore takes the 'a' indefinite article. While it is wrong to use 'n' for 'ng' in *length/strength* and so get *lenth/strenth*, the sound *lenkth/strenkth* is acceptable.

A long 'o' goes before 'll' in *poll* (vote) and before 'lt' in *revolt*, but there is a short 'o' in *resolve/dissolve/solve/golf* as in *doll*. *Either* as in *eye* or in *seize* – both are acceptable. *Envelope* starts -en as in end (-on is disliked by RP speakers). *Data* has a long first 'a'.

In formal speech, say before an audience, avoid dropping the 'r' if it is closely followed by another 'r' as in *deteriorate* to get deteriate: similarly, *February* can slip to Feburary, *temporary* to tempary (but temp'rary OK), *honorary* to honary (hon'rary is preferred), *itinerary* to itinery, *library* to libr'y, *probably* to prob'ly. Avoid dropping the fourth syllable in *particularly* to get particuly but the elision of the middle syllables of adjectives of four syllables ending in -*ary* makes the words easier to pronounce as in milit'ry, necess'ry.

Watch out for syllable elisions in *chocolate, police, mathematics* to get the sloppy choc'lte, p'lice, math'matics. Don't let *fifth* become fith, *months* drop to 'munce', *camera* to 'camra'; make *lure* rhyme with *pure* not 'poor'. Articulate *railway*: don't let it become 'ro-way'. Don't let *conflicts* sound like 'conflix'.

When speaking quickly, pronouns and auxiliary verbs easily disappear. Avoid *gonna/wanna, kinda, doncher* (don't you), *innit, wannit* (isn't it/ wasn't it), *'spec/'spose* (I expect/suppose). Careful speakers will retain the 't' in *facts, acts, ducts, pacts*; otherwise the listener hears fax/axe/ducks/packs. But it is silent in *often* as in *soften*.

American pronunciation differs markedly from the British. Some examples from the *Oxford Guide to English Usage*: the 'r' is sounded by American speakers wherever it is written, after vowels finally and before consonants, as well as before vowels like *burn, car, form*. The sound of *you* (as in *u, ew* spellings) after s, t, d, n, is replaced by the sound of *oo* as in resume (*resoom*), Tuesday (*Toosday*), due (*doo*), new (*noo*).

Americans pronounce asthma (*ass*-ma in RP) as *az*-ma; detour (*dee*-tour not *day*-tour in RP) as *de*-tour; *ga*la (*a* as in *calm* in RP) as *gale*. They will say *trow*ma as in *cow* whereas RP speakers will say *trau*ma (*au* as in *cause*).

Some forms of pronunciation are to be especially avoided. Among these are *Arctic* (do not drop the first 'c'); *et cetera* (not *eksetera*); don't let *garage* (with stress on the first syllable) sound like *garridge*; do not drop the first 'n' in *government* or the whole second syllable; do not say *pee* for pence in formal speech; avoid making *people* sound like *peeple*; ensure *plastic* rhymes with *fantastic*; *sovereignty* is pronounced *sov*'renty, not sounding like sov-*rain*-ty; a *suit* is now pronounced with an -*oo* sound although the *you* sound is still frequently heard. *Secretary* is pronounced *sek*-re-try (not *sek*-e-terry or even worse *sukk*-a-terry). *January* should sound like *Jan*-yoor-y, not Jan-yoo-ery (except in America). You take your pet to the *vet*-er-in-ary practice, not vet'nary. You buy jewel-ry not *joo-ler-y*. You look at a *pic*-ture not a *pitcher* and you make a *fort*-une, not a *forchoon*. And it is all a matter of pron*u*nciation, not pron*ou*nciation!

There are probably more regional forms of speech in the United Kingdom than anywhere else in the world, and it is in no sense suggested here that everyone should follow RP; adjustments have to be made as circumstances demand in various parts of the country. Just as much depends on *how* you say something as *what* you say. RP provides a useful guide.

Appendix 1: English grammar: some definitions

What is it? What does it do?

Brief definitions of the terminology used in English grammar are given here as a help in using this book. Examples are shown in brackets where appropriate.

Abbreviation: A shortened form of a word or phrase, company name, product or service. (*BBC, IPR, ad* for advertisement). No full stops between the characters nowadays.

Acronym: A word formed from a set of initials (*NATO*). No full stops.

Active voice: Attributes action of a verb to a person or thing from which it logically follows (the ship *is* sinking, the man *hits* the ball). Intransitive verbs can only occur in the active voice (the client *laughs*). See entry for verbs.

Adjectival noun: An adjective used as a noun (the *young*).

Adjective: Describes or qualifies a noun (a *big* firm).

Adverb: A word that qualifies or modifies a verb (drove *quickly*), an adjective (*terribly* bad) or another adverb (*very* sadly). Care needed in use and positioning. See later entry for split infinitive.

Apostrophe: A mark to indicate the possessive case (the *firm's* staff, *men's* shirts) and the omission of a letter or letters (*shan't, can't*), or contractions of words (*'phone*).

Article: Definite article is the name for *the*; indefinite for *a* and *an*.

Bracket: Paired typographical marks to denote word(s), phrase or sentence in parenthesis, usually round ( ). Square brackets [ ] denote words inserted by someone other than the author.

Case: The role of a noun or noun phrase in relation to other words in a clause or sentence (in the *boy's* knees, boy is in the genitive case; similarly *boy* is in singular case, *boys* plural).

Clause: Part of a complex sentence usually with its own subject and verb; three main types – nominal clause when functioning like a noun phrase (*the name of the game*); relative clause like an adjective (*the man you love*); or adverbial (don't do it *unless you're sure*). Inferior to a sentence, superior to a phrase.

Collective noun: A noun referring to a group of people or animals (*audience, committee, family, herd, staff, team, majority, parliament, the clergy, the public*). Whether it takes a plural or singular verb depends on whether the group is considered as a single unit or as a collection of individuals (the audience *was* in its place but *were* clapping madly, the family *is* large; the board *is* meeting, but *are* going out to lunch).

Conjunction: A connecting word to join two clauses, or words in the same clause (*and, but, or*); also for introducing a subordinate clause (*although, because, since*).

Consonants: Letters of the alphabet other than the vowels *a, e, i, o, u*.

Count nouns: Nouns that can be used with numerical values

(*book/books*) that can form a plural or be used with an indefinite article and usually refer to objects (*table, ship, pen*) as distinct from non-count nouns (*adolescence, richness, scaffolding*).

Dangling participle: Also called hanging participle, or dangler; a participle clause usually contains no subject and is unattached to the subject of the main clause. Considered ungrammatical rather than a style fault. (*Now broken, Fred Jones can remember what the teacup looked like.* Clearly, Mr Jones was not broken even though his memory was perfect.)

Determiners: Words that precede nouns to limit their meaning in some way (*all, both, this, every*).

Double negative: Two negative words in a sentence can confuse the reader. (I *haven't* got *nothing*; I *wouldn't* be surprised if they *didn't* come.)

Elision: Omission of speech sound or syllable as in w*r*ong, lis*t*en, hym*n*. In each example the elided character is italicized.

Ellipsis: Omission of word or words from speech or writing usually recoverable from the context; useful in formal contexts for avoiding repetition. (We are as keen *to help* as you are.) Ellipsis of *to help* avoids duplication, aids flow and sharpens style.

First person: Pronouns and determiners denoting the speaker or writer in contrast to the addressee or others. (*I, me, myself, my, mine* in the singular; *we, us, ourselves, our, ours* in the plural.)

Gender: Nouns and pronouns representing natural distinctions of sex. The masculine gender denotes persons and animals that are *male*; feminine, those that are *female*.

Genitive: The case of nouns and pronouns indicating possession of something or close association of something (possessive case, the *cat's* paws).

Headlinese: The grammar of newspaper headlines where articles and other words are omitted for reasons of space and where present tense verbs are used for past events (*soldier shoots terrorists*).

Hyphen: Mark to join words or to indicate word division, to separate figures or groups of figures. Many uses: in compound nouns as in *air-conditioning*, but *air force*; in compound adjectives as in a *two-page* report; with a prefix as in the votes have been *re-counted*.

Idiom: An expression with a meaning that cannot be guessed from the meaning of the individual words as in 'his mother *passed away* (died) this morning'. A peculiarity of expression or phraseology in language (*over the moon, under the weather*) which sounds natural to those born and bred in England, but incomprehensible to foreigners.

Indirect question: A question as reported in indirect speech. (*I asked when he could attend the meeting.*)

Infinitive: The form of a verb when used without direct relationship to time, person or number, often preceded by *to*. (*I wanted to laugh.*) See entry for split infinitive.

Interrogative: A word or sentence used to ask a question. (*What do you do?*)

Mass noun: Never takes the indefinite article *a* and seldom has a plural. (*Bread, capitalism, clothing, dust, equipment, leisure, traffic*).

Modal verbs: Auxiliary verbs to express mood (*can/could, may/ might, shall/should, will/would, must*).

Modifier: Words which modify other words: *very* + badly (adverb); *really* + useful (adjective).

Noun: The name of a person, place or thing whether material or immaterial, abstract or concrete. Inflects for plural and functions as subject or object of a sentence. Common nouns (*cat/car*) are distinct from proper nouns or names (names of people, cities, months, days of the week and which carry a capital initial letter).

Number: Contrasts between singular and plural; in nouns (*girl/ girls*), pronouns (*she/they*), verbs (*says/say; was/were*).

Object: The object of a sentence follows a verb and is normally a noun or noun phrase. (the car hit the *wall*; the car hit the *wall, bricks and all*).

Paragraph: A short passage in text, at the start of a fresh line of thought, sometimes (but not always) indented. A unit of thought, not of length.

Parenthesis: A word, clause or sentence inserted as an after-thought and marked off with brackets, commas or dashes as in 'This is a useful book (*it should be kept for reference*).' Plural *parentheses*.

Participle: A form of the verb normally ending in *-ing* or *-ed*. Present participle (*being, doing/is going/looking*); past participle (*been/done/has gone/looked*).

Passive voice: Where the object of the sentence 'receives' the action of the verb (fast drivers *will be prosecuted*). Only transitive verbs can have passive forms. See entry for verbs.

Person: Classifies whether pronouns and verbs indicate the speaker, the addressee or a third party as first, second or third person, singular or plural. (First person: *I am/we are going to the theatre*; second: *you are going to the theatre*; third: *he/they are going to the theatre*.)

Phrase: A short expression, a group of words of lesser weight than a clause forming a unit in itself; part of a sentence that is not the subject (I refuse *to do it*).

Plural: More than one (*cats and dogs*, but *sheep and deer*).

Possessive: A word or case indicating possession or ownership; the possessive case of nouns is also called the genitive case (*John's hands, girls' fingers*).

Predicate: That part of a sentence that is not the subject (I *decided what to do*).

Preposition: Words that relate word sets to each other and that generally precede the words they govern. Usually short words (*by, in, for, to, out, up*). Traditional prejudice against ending a sentence with a preposition is now fading, especially for informal contexts.

Pronoun: A word that replaces or stands for a noun without naming a person or thing already known mentioned from the context. (*I/you/they* asked a question, and sometimes replaces a clause as in Why did you ask *that?*)

Proper noun: A noun referring to a particular person, place, month, day of week, etc and carrying a capital initial letter (*Smith, London, March, Monday*).

Second person: Denotes the person addressed as distinct from the speaker or writer or other person (*you, yourself, yourselves*, etc).

Sentence: The largest unit in traditional grammar; a set of words complete in itself containing subject and predicate (all that part that is not the subject). Usually contains a verb; starts with a capital letter and ends with a full stop, and also with question or exclamation mark. (*The client heard a presentation.*) Where *the client* is the subject, *heard* the verb and *presentation* the object.

Singular: A word or form referring to a single person or thing.

Split infinitive: Where an adverb is placed between *to* and the infinitive form of a verb (*to boldly go*). Nowadays it's considered a myth that *to* must never be detached from the verb. Generally, it is better not to split but avoidance can sometimes cause awkward constructions. ('Do you want *to* really help them?' is preferable to putting *really* before *to*, impossible after *help*.)

Subject: That part of the sentence which usually comes first and governs the verb, often defined as the 'doer' of the verbal action. See entry above for sentence.

Syllable: Unit of pronunciation; a word or part of a word uttered with a single pulse of the voice and usually containing one vowel sound with or without consonant(s) preceding or following it. *Pro/nun/ci/a/tion* has five syllables.

Synonym: A word or phrase having the same meaning (or virtually the same) as another. Some synonyms for *care* are (nouns) *anxiety, caution, charge, burden*; (verbs) *be anxious, be disposed, have regard*.

Tense: A form taken by the verb in a sentence to indicate the time at which the action is viewed as occurring. Past (something that *has happened*), present (*is happening*) and future (*will happen*) tenses. In media usage, present tenses can refer to the past (PRO *resigns*).

Third person: Denotes the person or persons spoken or written about as distinct from the addressee, speaker or writer (*he, him, they, theirs*, etc).

Verb: The core of a sentence or clause, the 'doing' or 'action' word. Major types are transitive, intransitive, auxiliary. Using a transitive verb, the meaning passes from subject to the object of the sentence (he *built* the house); using an intransitive verb the meaning is complete without the addition of an object (she *laughs*). Auxiliary verbs form tenses, moods and voices of other verbs (*be, do, have*) and modals (*may, might* etc). Verbless, or incomplete, sentences are common in sports commentaries and in broadcasting (*And now the news*).

Voice: Mode of inflecting verbs as being active or passive (the cat *ate* the food; the food *was eaten* by the cat).

Vowels: Letters of the alphabet producing simple vocal sound by continuous passage of breath (*a, e, i, o, u*). All English words contain at least one vowel.

Note: Source material for Appendices 1 and 2 has been drawn largely from the 1994 edition of the *Oxford Dictionary of English Grammar* and from the 1974 edition of the *Concise Oxford Dictionary* by permission of the Oxford University Press.

Appendix 2: Confusing pairs of words

Lookalikes: differences and distinctions

Many pairs of words look and sound alike, but some are exact opposites, while others have different shades of meaning. Get them wrong and you could have a verbal disaster on your hands: at best an embarrassing telephone call to rectify what is really meant, at worst a press release or print job that has to be corrected and reissued. Here are some of them.

Adaption/adaptation: While both mean the same thing, adaptation is preferred. Adaption is eventually expected to supplant adaptation which is slowly on the way out.

Alternate/alternative: Alternate as a verb means interchanging one thing with another; as a noun it means things of two kinds coming one after the other. Alternative as an adjective means offering choice between two things; as a noun denotes an option to choose between two or more things.

Biennial/biannual: Biennial means once every two years,

biannual twice a year or if preferred, twice yearly. Similarly, bimonthly means every two months, not twice a month. With this pair, it is often better to write it out in full rather than risk ambiguity.

Brochure/pamphlet: A brochure is normally taken to mean a wire-stitched or square-backed, illustrated colour-printed production used for promoting an organization's products, services or activities. There is little difference between a pamphlet, usually just a folded sheet produced in large numbers at low cost, and a leaflet.

Complement(ary)/compliment(ary): The former means completing, supplying a deficiency, two or more things complementing each other; the latter an expression of regard or praise as in 'with compliments'.

Compose/comprise: Compose means to constitute, to form or make up a list by putting two or more things or parts together, comprise means to include or contain the items on the list.

Delusion/illusion: A delusion denotes a false idea, impression or belief as a symptom of insanity, someone who is genuinely convinced of what is not the case (*a delusion of grandeur*); an illusion denotes a false impression as to the true nature of an object, a misapprehension of a true state of affairs (*an optical illusion*).

Derisive/derisory: Derisive means mocking, scoffing; derisory equals ridiculous, laughingly inefficient.

Especial(ly)/ special(ly): Little difference. Especial the adjective now replaced by special without much trouble; especially/specially the adverbs expected to survive in contexts where *in particular*, or *even more* is meant.

Disinterested/uninterested: The former suggests impartial or unbiased while the latter means indifference. Most writers prefer to write 'lack of interest' rather than disinterested.

Effect/affect: Effect means to accomplish something; affect means to have an influence upon something. The difficulty is compounded by the fact that both can be used as nouns and verb, although *affect* is more commonly used as a verb and *effect* as a noun.

Flout/flaunt: To flout means to violate a rule, show a contemptuous disregard; to flaunt means to show off, to make an ostentatious or defiant display.

Forgo/forego: To forgo is to abstain from or do without; to forego is to precede in place or time.

Fortuitous/fortunate: fortuitous means by accident or chance; fortunate equals lucky.

Imply/infer: To imply is to hint or state something; to infer is to draw a conclusion from what has been implied. A useful rule to remember is that the writer or speaker *implies*, while the reader or listener *infers*.

Inapt/inept: The former means not apt or unsuitable, the latter unskilful.

Less/fewer: The distinction between these words is often lost: *less* goes with singular 'mass' nouns (population/difficulty) while *fewer* with numbers or quantities capable of being counted or listed (people/things).

Magazine/journal: Both are periodicals, but a journal is usually the more serious, professional publication, like the *Journal* of the IPR.

Masterful/masterly: Masterful means domineering, wilful; masterly means executed with superior skill.

Number/amount: These two words are very close in definition, but be careful to distinguish between them: the distinction is whether they go with 'count' or 'mass' nouns, as in the *number* of releases sent out compared with the *amount* of work in writing them. As in this example, *number* is usually constructed with a plural.

Practical/practicable: Practical (suitable for use) and practicable (able to be done). What for example, is practical is to mail 100 news releases before the office closes, but not necessarily practicable in that there may not be the staff to do it.

Refute/deny: Both verbs dispute the truthfulness of a statement; deny says it is false, refute proves that it is.

Regretfully/regrettably: The former means an expression of regret, the latter something to be regretted, unwelcome, worthy of reproof.

Scotch/Scottish: Scotch is for whisky made in Scotland (-ey for varieties made in Ireland and the USA); Scottish for those from north of the Border.

That/which: Again close and often interchangeable pronouns. The important distinction between them is that *which* can never refer to people. *That* defines as in 'the PR firm that was formed', while *which* describes as in 'the PR firm, which was formed in 1990, is still operating profitably'. The careful observer will note that *which* usually follows a comma, while *that* doesn't need one before it.

Under/underneath: While there is a slim distinction between them, the simplest way to show it is to write *underneath* meaning 'directly covered by' while *under* means below or beneath. A sentence can end with *underneath* far more easily than it can with *under*.

Note: Further examples of confusing pairs will be found in the *Oxford Guide to English Usage*.

Further reading

Aitchison, James (1994) *Guide to Written English*, BCA by arrangement with Cassell, London.

Allen, RE (1990) *The Oxford Spelling Dictionary*, Oxford University Press

Allen, RE (1996) *The Oxford Writers' Dictionary*, Oxford University Press.

Amis, Kingsley (1997) *The King's English. A Guide to Modern Usage*, HarperCollins, London.

Blamires, Harry (1994) *The Queen's English*, Bloomsbury, London.

Bryson, Bill (1984) *Penguin Dictionary of Troublesome Words*, Penguin, London.

Burchfield, RW (ed.) *(1996) Fowler's Modern English Usage*, Oxford University Press.

Burchfield, Robert (1981) *The Spoken Word, A BBC Guide*, British Broadcasting Corporation, London.

Cutts, Martin (1995) *The Plain English Guide*, Oxford University Press.

Dummett, Michael (1993) *Grammar & Style for examination candidates and others*, Duckworth, London.

Gowers, Sir Ernest (1987) *The Complete Plain Words*, Penguin, London.

Hart's Rules for Compositors and Readers (1983) Oxford University Press.

Kahn, John Ellison (1985) *The Right Word at the Right Time*, Reader's Digest Association, London.

Kahn, John Ellison (1991) *How to Write and Speak Better*, Reader's Digest Association, London.

Marshall, Susie B (1991) *Collins Gem Dictionary of Spelling and Word Division*, HarperCollins, London.

Montague-Smith, Patrick (1992) *Debrett's Correct Form*, Headline Book Publishing, London.

Partridge, Eric (1973) (ed. Janet Whitcut 1994) *Usage and Abusage*, BCA by arrangement with Hamish Hamilton, London.

Partridge, Eric (1978) *A Dictionary of Clichés*, Routledge, London.

Soule, Richard (1991) *The Penguin Dictionary of English Synonyms*, Penguin, London.

Strunk, William and White, E B (1979) *The Elements of Style*, Allyn and Bacon, Needham Heights, Mass.

The Economist Style Guide (1993) Hamish Hamilton in association with Economist Books, London.

The Times Guide to English Style and Usage (1992) Times Books, a Division of HarperCollins, London.

Waterhouse, Keith (1993) *Waterhouse on Newspaper Style*, Penguin, London.

Weiner, ESC and Delanhunty, Andrew (1994) *The Oxford Guide to English Usage*, Oxford University Press.

Note: There are very many books and guides available on style, including several published by newspapers for their own staff, for the reader to consult. The titles in this bibliography, and others mentioned and acknowledged, form a selection recommended by the author to be of special interest and use in day-to-day writing and editing.

Index

Index